COMEBACK KIDS

THE PENGUINS RETURN TO GLORY AND WIN THE 2009 STANLEY CUP

TRIUMPH
BOOKS

Pittsburgh Post-Gazette®

Penguins players celebrate after defeating Detroit in Game 7 of the Stanley Cup final.

This book is available in quantity at special discounts for your group or organization.
For further information contact:

Triumph Books
542 South Dearborn Street
Suite 750
Chicago, IL 60605
Phone: (312) 939-3330
Fax: (312) 663-3557

Printed in the United States of America
ISBN: 978-1-60078-339-5

All photographs courtesy of the Pittsburgh Post-Gazette, except where otherwise indicated

Content packaged by Mojo Media, Inc.
Joe Funk: Editor
Jason Hinman: Creative Director

Pittsburgh Post-Gazette
John Robinson Block, Co-publisher and Editor-in-Chief
David M. Shribman, Executive Editor and Vice-President
Susan L. Smith, Managing Editor
Mary C. Leonard, Deputy Managing Editor
Jerry Micco, Assistant Managing Editor, Sports

BOOK EDITOR
Donna Eyring, Sports Editor

PHOTOGRAPHERS
Peter Diana, Bob Donaldson, Lake Fong, Matt Freed, John Heller, Michael Henninger,
Marlene Karras, Steve Mellon, Robin Rombach, Andy Starnes

PHOTO EDITORS
Larry Roberts, Joyce Mendelsohn

ADMINISTRATIVE COORDINATOR
Allison Alexander, Marketing Manager

contents

FOREWORD

And so another season, another championship. Ho hum. In a remarkable four month period, teams from the city of Pittsburgh – a Rust Belt community with no signs of rust in its civic pride, an old city inspired by the exploits of its young athletes, a place in America's interior whose sports teams have a cherished place in America's heart – twice have emerged as champions.

First, a Super Bowl, the Steelers' sixth. And now a Stanley Cup championship, the Penguins' third.

Eat your heart out Cleveland, which may have LeBron James but lacks a hockey team or even a single Super Bowl appearance. Retire to the sidelines, Detroit, which no longer owns the Stanley Cup and has a football team that didn't win a single game last year. Look west for inspiration, New York, for your two baseball teams, two basketball teams, two football teams and two hockey teams together have not won as many championships in the entire 21st century as Pittsburgh has in the winter and spring of 2009.

Pittsburgh, city of champions. Again.

This time, with feeling. This time, as metaphor.

For in truth these Stanley Cup Penguins are a metaphor for the ages. A team counted out but roaring back. A team that is young and hip, or at least accomplished in the hip check, which on the ice is even more important. A team that honors the colorful past but reaches to a promising future.

These Penguins–comeback artists, youthful faces of an old city, steeped in a rich and revered heritage – *are* Pittsburgh.

Which is why their ascension has been so interesting, so thrilling, so utterly irresistible.

The last two seasons they started slowly, as if their potential was just that – potential, but not enough to produce points. Then there was a deep, almost primeval, stirring, in their souls and in the city that has stood by them in times terrible and triumphant. And finally the emergence of a team so skilled, so indomitable, so inspiring, that it captured the attention of hockey fans beyond Pittsburgh and of Pittsburgers who thought they were beyond the reach of hockey's allure.

Pittsburgh, the ultimate football town, became Pittsburgh, the marquis hockey town.

To a list that includes Toronto, Montreal, Minneapolis, Boston and Detroit, you can, confidently and permanently, add Pittsburgh. Here we do not sit in an arena befuddled by the mysteries of the offside rule. Here we know slashing when we see it (though never when it's called against the Penguins). Here we know the virtues of roughing (though not when the other guys do it). Here we know icing, as in the phrase: *The Pens' Stanley Cup is the icing on Pittsburgh's 2009 sports season.*

If Pittsburgh now stands among the great hockey towns of North America, it is because these current Penguins stand on the shoulders of giants. Scotty

Bowman. Leo Boivin. Paul Coffey. Ron Francis. Larry Murphy. Bryan Trottier. Craig Patrick. Jaromir Jagr. (Are we allowed to utter his name in Pittsburgh?)

And need we mention Bob Johnson and Herb Brooks? And the peerless Mario Lemieux?

A decade, a generation, from now, some future Penguins champions will surely add the names Sidney Crosby, Evgeni Malkin, Marc-Andre Fleury. And Dan Bylsma. Who will ever omit Dan Bylsma from the very top tier of Penguins greats?

These Penguins' hometowns have a special kind of hockey poetry: Kiev and Cole Harbour, Sorel and Sault Ste. Marie, Chelyabinsk and Topolcany, and of course Thunder Bay. (Every championship team needs someone from Thunder Bay, home of Alex Delvecchio, Eric Staal, Marc Staal, Jared Staal…and our own Jordan Staal.) Plus there's Worcester, Mass., and Concord, Mass., just to prove that the Stanley Cup champions have some domestic content. But these Pens are most at home here, in Pittsburgh, and in the lousiest, darkest, smallest, oldest and maybe greatest arena in all of civilization, or hockey, which in Pittsburgh means the same thing. For the Pens, a team with no super-ego, the Igloo is the id.

A shiny new arena is going up right in the shadow of the old barn on Centre Avenue but in truth there hasn't been an empty seat at a Penguins game since forever and probably won't be another one for forever. The Pens are a hot ticket in both senses of the word. How hot? Hot enough to be named one of the fastest-growing brands in sports by Forbes magazine, the Sports Illustrated of the economic elite.

You could sense this Penguins fever on the streets of Pittsburgh, where increasing numbers of people are wearing the black and gold (or the powder blue) of the Pens. You could see it on women's ears, where suddenly Penguins earrings sprouted, or on their wrists, where Penguins bracelets find a comfortable home. (Who cares if they were purchased at the Aviary? They're on message, and in style). You could see it outside Mellon Arena, where thousands came together—a gathering of the tribe, you might say—to watch a giant screen version of the Pens game, a kind of outdoor festival of hockey hokum.

So now the Stanley Cup is back in Pittsburgh, where it belongs, and Pittsburgh is recognized as the hockey hotbed it has become. We're growing our own players here—check those college rosters and you will see that I am right—and we are growing a hockey tradition as unique as the Pittsburgh salad, or as distinctive as the pierogi wrap. We're comfortable in those Pens jerseys. They suit us well.

The day after the Pens swept the Carolina Hurricanes the Post-Gazette led the front page with a giant headline reading *Extraordinary journey to the top.* The headline appeared over a story on President Obama's introduction of Judge Sonia Sotomayor to the nation. You might be forgiven if you thought that headline was meant for the local hockey team instead of the Supreme Court in Washington. Extraordinary journey, indeed. And we—all of us—were along for the ride.

—By David M. Shribman
Executive Editor, Pittsburgh Post-Gazette

CHAMPS

Penguins win third Cup in thriller

June 12, 2009 • By Dave Molinari

It was said that the Detroit Red Wings could not lose Game 7 of a Stanley Cup final on home ice. They did. That Marc-Andre Fleury could not be counted on to win big games. He has.

That these Penguins were not ready to be champions. They are.

They defeated the Red Wings, 2-1, in Game 7 at Joe Louis Arena to earn the third Stanley Cup in franchise history.

The driving forces behind the victory were forward Max Talbot, who scored both goals, and Fleury, who turned aside 23 of 24 shots and made a lunging game-, season- and Cup-saving stop on Nicklas Lidstrom with about a second to play.

Penguins center Evgeni Malkin, who led the playoffs in scoring with 36 points, received the Conn Smythe Trophy as the most valuable player in the postseason.

"He told us before the playoffs that he was going to lead us to the Stanley Cup," right winger Bill Guerin said. "He's an amazing competitor, an amazing player."

But this victory was not about one guy, or two or three. Championships are won by 20 or 21 or 22 men, although the Penguins had to get by with 19 for much of last night.

Captain Sidney Crosby missed most of the final 34-plus minutes after Detroit's Johan Franzen hit him at center ice early in the second period, pinning Crosby's left knee between his own and the boards.

Crosby went to the dressing room and did not return until the start of the third and managed only one 32-second shift in the middle of that period.

"We tried to make it so I couldn't feel it anymore, but it just didn't work," he said.

The injury did not, however, prevent him from becoming the youngest captain in league history to hoist the Stanley Cup.

"It's everything you dream of," Crosby said. "It's an amazing feeling."

He later pronounced himself to be "100 percent" for the victory parade.

Crosby was the No. 2 scorer in these playoffs, putting up 31 points in 24 games.

Talbot gave the Penguins all the offense they needed, but it was not clear that he had the winner until Fleury threw himself across the crease to deny Lidstrom on a rebound with about a second to go.

"I saw the shot coming in, and I just tried to do everything I could to get over there," Fleury said.

He did and, in the process, secured a championship and shattered the perception that he cannot produce when the pressure and stakes are highest.

"It's only fitting that he made that save with a second

left to clinch it for us," defenseman Mark Eaton said. "You can't say enough about the way he's played, and what he did for us."

Winning Game 7 avenged losing the Cup to Detroit at Mellon Arena in 2008 and completed a remarkable turn-around by the Penguins. When Dan Bylsma was brought in to replace Michel Therrien as coach Feb. 15, they were five points out of the final playoff spot in the Eastern Conference standings.

Bylsma promptly led them to an 18-3-4 record during the stretch drive and rallied them from a 3-2 deficit in this series. He joins Al MacNeil as the only rookie coaches to win a Cup after getting his job during the season. MacNeil did it with Montreal in 1971.

The Penguins have won all three of their Cups on the road – they did it in Minnesota in 1991 and in Chicago in 1992 – and last night became the only road team to win a game in this series.

The loss was just the Red Wings' second in 14 home dates during the playoffs and marked just the third time in 15 tries that the visiting club has won Game 7 in a Cup final.

It helped that the Penguins never had to play from behind. Talbot gave them a 1-0 lead at 1:13 of the second when he put a shot between the legs of Red Wings goalie Chris Osgood from the inner edge of the right circle. Malkin made the goal possible by getting his stick on a Brad Stuart pass and deflecting it to Talbot.

Talbot beat Osgood on a two-on-one break at 10:07 of the second, and that provided the Penguins' margin of victory after Detroit's Jonathan Ericsson scored from the right point at 13:53 of the third.

But that was the only puck Detroit got past Fleury, and at 10:37 p.m., the Penguins triggered a civic celebration that might last for days.

"I really don't know if it's sunk in yet," Eaton said. "It doesn't get any better than this." ■

Maxime Talbot scores the first of his two goals against the Red Wings' Chris Osgood in the second period of Game 7.

Penguins owner Mario Lemieux celebrates with Evgeni Malkin after winning the Cup against the Red Wings.

PENGUINS
knock out
Red Wings

June 12, 2009 • By Ron Cook

Facing overwhelming odds as the road team in a Stanley Cup final Game 7, in throbbing Joe Louis Arena filled with 20,000-plus red-clad fanatics, including legendary Muhammad Ali decked out in the home team's red jersey, the Penguins took the Detroit Red Wings' best punch and earned — I mean, *earned* — the right to be called champions forever.

The big, blood-thirsty crowd saw its knockout, all right.

The mighty Red Wings went down for the count.

"Time after time, I think our team has proven that we're a true team," Penguins captain Sidney Crosby said. "This is an amazing feeling."

It's hard to say what was more impressive about the 2-1 victory — that the Penguins played nearly all of the final two periods without the injured Crosby (knee), that goaltender Marc-Andre Fleury stood tall and stopped all but one Detroit shot in a building where he had fished 11 pucks out from his net in the first three games of the series or that big-time, big-game forward Max Talbot scored the first two goals in the second period to send the team on to the Cup and immortality. It's not important, really. All that matters is that all of

Pittsburgh gets to enjoy this remarkable accomplishment by a very special hockey club.

Champions forever, indeed.

"This is why I came back," said defenseman Brooks Orpik, who turned down the chance to make more elsewhere to re-sign with the Penguins after last season.

And the guy who chose not to come back?

You knew I'd get to Marian Hossa, didn't you?

As fun as the game was to watch, the most enjoyable part came afterward when the boys lined up to accept congratulatory handshakes from the proud but beaten Red Wings, including Hossa, who had abandoned them after last season because he didn't think they were good enough to win a championship.

Do you think Crosby, Fleury, Talbot and the rest enjoyed being on their side of the Hossa handshake?

But this win — this terrific championship, the third in franchise history — wasn't about what Hossa didn't do. It was about what the Penguins did.

They were phenomenal, winning the final two games of a series that was nothing but intense from start to finish.

The 2-1 victory in Game 6 at Mellon Arena was

Maxime Talbot is congratulated by teammates Chris Kunitz and Tyler Kennedy after scoring against the Red Wings in the second period of Game 7.

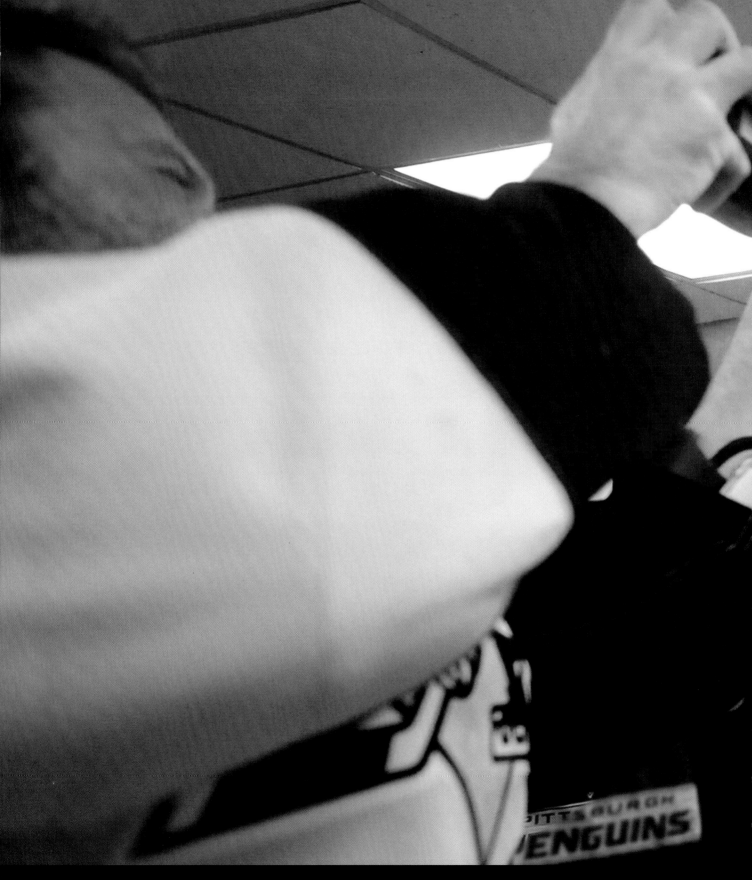

Sidney Crosby is sprayed by Sergei Gonchar after winning the Cup.

wonderful, but all that did was give the Penguins the chance to play Game 7. The site: The Joe, a rink that had brutally demonized them in this Cup final and the one a year ago when the Red Wings were the better team and took the Cup in six games.

But the Penguins never blinked. Not staring down the Red Wings, the home crowd or those long odds against them. Only two road teams in NHL history had won a Game 7 for the Cup. No road team in any sport had won a title since the 1979 Pirates beat the Baltimore Orioles at old Memorial Stadium.

I'm sure I don't have to tell you that's a long time ago.

Mid-February seems like ages ago, too.

It was Feb. 15 that Penguins general manager Ray Shero fired coach Michel Therrien and replaced him with Wilkes-Barre/Scranton coach Dan Bylsma. The team was five points out of a playoff spot with 25 games to play. All might not have been hopeless, but it sure seemed that way at the time.

But the Penguins went a stunning, 18-3-4 down the stretch. They took out the hated Philadelphia Flyers in six games in the first round of the playoffs.. They survived the great Alex Ovechkin and his Washington Capitals in seven games, winning the final one on the road, 6-2. They turned all of Carolina blue with a four-game sweep in the Eastern Conference final.

And then down Detroit went.

"Where we've come since last year at this time, since the start of the season, since Feb. 15, wherever you want to pick up the story line, it's an amazing thing to have accomplished and earned," Bylsma said.

That the Penguins finished the job basically without Crosby merely added to their legend. Crosby was hurt early in the second period after a nasty collision along the boards with Detroit's Johan Franzen.

"Sid has bailed us out a million times," winger Bill Guerin said. "It was our time to get the job done for him."

No problem.

Not with Talbot, who scored those two beautiful second-period goals. Sure, he had dreamed as a kid of scoring the winning goal in a Game 7. But two? I mean, whose dreams are that exotic?

"I don't think I ever dreamed of scoring two goals in an NHL game!" Talbot gushed. "This is the best day of my life."

Fleury made the 2-0 lead stand up by making 23 saves. Never again will the man have to hear that he is not a big-time goaltender.

"I'm so happy about that," said Talbot, perhaps Fleury's closest friend. After being pulled in the second period of the 5-0 loss in Game 5, Fleury bounced back to allow just a single goal in each of the final two pressurized games. Right to the end, the Red Wings challenged him. Literally, as the final second ticked off, he said no to Detroit captain Nicklas Lidstrom's great scoring chance.

So ends the Red Wings' run as Stanley Cup champions.

The Penguins are the NHL's new kings.

All hail the new kings. ■

Red Wings' goaltender Chris Osgood stops a shot by the Penguins' Sidney Crosby in the first period of Game 3 at Mellon Arena.

(opposite) Penguins goalie Marc-Andre Fleury makes a save on the Red Wings' Darren Helm in the third period of Game 2. (above) Evgeni Malkin lifts the Conn Smythe Award after defeating Detroit in Game 7.

It's a great day for Penguins

July 23, 2005 • By Ron Cook

It's still the Steelers' town, make no mistake. It's always going to be the Steelers' town. But you know what's really cool? It's no longer just the Steelers' town.

You remember the Penguins? If you think hard enough, they'll surely come to mind. Here's a hint: They play hockey at Mellon Arena. At least they did before the NHL shut down its dying game almost a year ago and went away, looking for a miracle that would make it healthy.

Well, the Penguins are back.

Back in a big way.

Actually, back and resurrected from the dead in an almost unfathomable way.

The guess here is the late, great Badger Bob Johnson wouldn't take the least bit offense from Penguins president Ken Sawyer intentionally ratcheting up his trademark slogan yesterday by gushing, "It's a spectacular day for hockey!"

Official ratification of the NHL's new collective bargaining agreement in New York by the league's owners would have been enough. That gives the Penguins and their small-market ilk a fairly even chance to compete with the big-market bullies in New York, Detroit and Philadelphia. That's why the arenas were dark last season. That's why all of the long, cold, boring winter nights were worth it.

Without that new CBA, hockey wouldn't survive here, at least not for the long haul. The Penguins, exactly like the Pirates in baseball's economic chaos, couldn't afford to compete. They had to give away their top players. Jaromir Jagr. Ron Francis. Alexei Kovalev. Martin Straka. They didn't just miss the Stanley Cup playoffs in the three previous years there was hockey. They had the worst record in the league in 2003-04. The Pirates can survive last place year after year after year because it's baseball on a pleasant Saturday summer night at beautiful PNC Park for a fairly reasonable price. The Penguins can't because it's hockey on a Tuesday night in January against Calgary at aging Mellon Arena for a fairly outrageous price. That's why when they turned the lights out in the old building after the last hockey game in 2004, you had to wonder if they'd ever turn them on again, or maybe you didn't care if they did or, at the very least, you asked, what's the point?

Thankfully, that question is now moot.

And this day was so much more spectacular.

The pucks might not have bounced the Penguins' way recently, but their draft lottery ball certainly did.

When it popped out first, it couldn't have had a more magical name on it.

Sidney Crosby.

A superstar in junior hockey and a household name in Canada long before his draft year, Sidney Crosby was instantly hailed as the on-ice savior of the Penguins. Lesser competitors may have shied away from the expectations, but Crosby has met and exceeded all of the wildest wants of the Penguins fan base.

"We filled a need today," Penguins general manager Craig Patrick would say later.

"For a forward who can score goals and make plays and be a superstar, that's all."

Like Sawyer, Patrick didn't need a plane to get home from New York.

This wasn't like when the Steelers picked Ben Roethlisberger No. 1 in the 2004 NFL draft. The team still had Tommy Maddox at quarterback. Big Ben would have to wait his turn. Or so we thought.

This also wasn't like when the Pirates picked Barry Bonds No. 1 in the 1985 baseball amateur draft. He would need a brief time in the minors and — let's be honest here — wouldn't really become a truly legendary player until he started dabbling with the clear and the cream, unintentionally or otherwise.

Crosby, at least based on potential, is unlike any athlete to come to Pittsburgh.

"People have said he's got the vision of Wayne Gretzky and the goal-scoring and play-making ability of Mario Lemieux," Patrick said.

Not even the fabulous Lemieux was this heavily hyped when he joined the Penguins in 1984. This is the Information Age. There was no Internet then, no round-the-clock talk radio, no satellite television to instantly beam sporting events from every corner of the world into our living rooms. Hockey people around the planet have known of Crosby for years. A lot of scouts will tell you he was better, at 16, than the top two players taken in the draft, Alexander Ovechkin and

Penguins property Evgeni Malkin.

But if the expectations on Crosby will be stifling, he'll have advantages that Lemieux didn't, advantages that should keep him a fan favorite. One, he speaks the language. Two, he comes across as personable and likable. And three, he joins a much different last-place team than Lemieux did. The '84 team had no real players and no hope. Today's Penguins have Lemieux and Mark Recchi. They have their goaltender of the future, Marc-Andre Fleury, the No. 1 overall pick of the 2003 draft. Soon, they might have Malkin.

"It's inconceivable that this team would be allowed to leave town, with the team we're going to have for the next 20 years," Sawyer said.

That was a not-so-subtle shot at the local politicos who have been dragging their feet with the new arena the Penguins need to stay here beyond 2007. There was little pressure on them to get the thing built before the NHL's new CBA and before the team got lucky beyond its wildest dreams with Crosby. There will be tremendous pressure on them if the kid and the old guy — sorry, Mario — make the team a Stanley Cup contender again.

Who would have guessed that during those horrible winter nights when Mellon Arena was dark and the Penguins were gone and all but forgotten? ■

Crosby was an instant hit in the NHL, racking up 102 points and finishing sixth in the league in scoring. He waited only until the next year to grab the reins of the entire league, setting the pace with an impressive 36 goals and 84 assists to win the Art Ross Trophy and become the youngest player in any major professional sport to lead his league in scoring.

adversity, is signed, sealed, and delivered

September 6, 2006 • By Shelly Anderson

t took Russian center Evgeni Malkin more than 26 months and some tense moments to get to Pittsburgh from the time the Penguins drafted him second overall in 2004.

It took him about 15 hours to get a sense of what life can be like for an NHL star – off the ice, anyway.

There was his arrival at Pittsburgh International, where he signed autographs and was met by a handful of reporters. There was dinner that night at Hall of Fame player and team owner Mario Lemieux's house, where Malkin joined, among others, general manager Ray Shero and players Sidney Crosby and Sergei Gonchar for filet mignon, lobster and a tour of a home full of memorabilia and trophies.

There was his first trip to Mellon Arena, with sights along the way pointed out, including the two North Shore stadiums.

There was the signing of his Penguins rookie contract, three years at $984,200 per year plus incentive bonuses that could top $2 million, followed by a news conference with plenty of lights and clicking cameras.

Malkin, 20, who speaks very little English, watched intently as the team played a promotional highlight video of some of his more spectacular goals.

He answered several questions through interpreter Olga McQueen, looking at the questioners but showing little emotion. His few smiles came during the photo ops, when he was presented a No. 71 Penguins jersey by Lemieux and when he posed with others.

The difficult journey is over for Malkin. The Penguins and his agents, J.P. Barry and Pat Brisson, remain braced for a legal battle with his Russian team, Magnitogorsk Metallurg, which could contest Malkin playing in the NHL.

Malkin's long transition had started about a month before, when Metallurg, his hometown team in the Russian Super League, pressured him into signing a one-year contract in the wee hours of the morning.

"The next day, after I signed the contract, I was very upset and I looked forward to leaving as soon as I could," Malkin said. "That's why I phoned J.P. Barry and asked for help."

Barry met Malkin when the player slipped away from Metallurg at the Helsinki, Finland, airport. The two remained there five days until Malkin could get a visa to travel to the United States.

"The team was training only 10 miles away, and we were only 1 kilometer from the Russian embassy,"

Once all the hurdles were leapt and Evgeni Malkin was able to come to the NHL, he wasted no time in becoming a superstar. Despite speaking little English and coming to a culture he knew next to nothing about, Malkin had no problems adjusting to the international language of hockey. He scored in his first NHL game and didn't look back in 2006-07, winning the Calder Trophy.

Barry said. "We needed to get to the American embassy to get the visa, so we were basically going right by the Russian embassy walking down the road. We had to be quiet and subtle about what we were doing."

Some considered Malkin missing, and there were some fears about his safety or that of his parents in Magnitogorsk.

"When I was in Helsinki, I definitely was a bit concerned, but not that much," Malkin said. "I had the feeling, knowing Mr. [Gennady] Velichkin [general director of Metallurg] for so many years, he wouldn't go for any harsh measures."

Once he got the visa, Malkin flew to Los Angeles and trained there with NHL players. He said he was able to reassure his parents and help soothe bitter fans.

"I can understand my fans pretty well," he said. "When I signed the contract with Magnitogorsk, they felt very happy about me staying in Russia and playing with the club. But after what happened, I'm sure they were upset.

"Later on, I got a chance to call a few friends of mine and explain what was going on, that I was happy about my decision and that it was my dream to come here and play with the Pittsburgh Penguins club. I was always open about my desire to come to North America. My friends understood me, and now I keep in touch with them and my family in Russia. I know that everything will calm down."

And Malkin (his first name is yev-GEN-ee with a hard "G") can get on with his career. Malkin, 6 feet 3 and 192 pounds, has the size and deceptive speed reminiscent of Lemieux, but he also has a strong physical side to his play.

"With his reach and his size, he's got a lot of talent," said Lemieux, who looked to be a hair taller than the newest Penguin.

Lemieux understands the transition Malkin faces.

"I told him that I didn't speak any English until I came to Pittsburgh," said Lemieux, a native of Montreal who was the first overall draft pick in 1984. "I'm the perfect example that you can make it work. I know it's going to take some time, the first year or so, to get acclimated to a new culture, but I'm sure he'll do fine."

Malkin will live with Gonchar, a Russian-born Penguins defenseman.

Shero hopes that will help Malkin be as comfortable as possible and vowed to do whatever it takes to help him thrive.

"Going through what he did to come over, the commitment and courage he showed, makes us feel very good about him," Shero said. ■

He may not fly as gracefully as Superman, but Malkin is a true superhero on the ice. The runner up for the Hart Trophy in 2008, he led the NHL in scoring with 113 points in 2009 to capture the Art Ross Trophy.

At
HEAVEN'S
GATE

Life after a run at the Cup

September 28, 2008 • By Dave Molinari

Don't get the wrong idea. History doesn't completely rule out the possibility of the Penguins winning the Stanley Cup in 2009.

It just comes awfully close.

Oh, the Penguins can be encouraged to learn that there is, in fact, precedent for a team winning the championship a year after losing in the Cup final. Especially if they don't notice that it's only happened once since the NHL expanded from six to 12 teams in 1967. The Edmonton Oilers did it in 1984, beating the New York Islanders in five games in the championship round after being swept by the same opponent a year earlier. So when the Penguins, who lost the 2008 final to Detroit in six games, open the 2008-09 season with a pair of games against Ottawa in Stockholm, Sweden next weekend, they will begin trying to fight their way into one of pro hockey's most exclusive clubs. They've been compared to the Oilers of the early- and mid-1980s frequently during the past few winters — it's hard to miss the parallels between a team built around the likes of Wayne Gretzky, Mark Messier, and Grant Fuhr and one with Sidney Crosby, Evgeni Malkin, and Marc-Andre Fleury in its nucleus — and now will try to claim a space in the record book where only the Oilers' signature has been scrawled.

That seems an awful lot to ask of any club, but Ed Johnston, who was the Penguins' general manager when the Oilers were dominating the NHL, believes these Penguins could pull it off.

"We have a lot of similarities here," said Johnston, now a senior adviser with the Penguins. "You look at the youth and talent we have, with Crosby and Malkin and [Jordan] Staal, and our young [defense]. "We've got the guy in nets, almost like Fuhr. If you're making a comparison, I think that's a pretty good comparison."

When Edmonton went from second place to league champion in 12 months, Ronald Reagan was running for his second term as president.

"Hello," by Lionel Richie was the No. 1 song on the Billboard charts.

"The Natural," starring Robert Redford, was filling theaters across the country.

A promising center named Mario Lemieux was three weeks away from being the No. 1 choice in the NHL draft.

Sidney Crosby was more than three years from being born.

The Penguins can't deny those realities, but aren't fixating on them, either.

"I don't [care] about it," center Max Talbot said,

"because I know we can win."

Crosby is no less optimistic, as is his nature, but offered a more measured response when asked about the fate that have befallen most Cup runners-up, and how to avoid it.

"I haven't played the next year after going to the Stanley Cup final yet, so I wouldn't be able to tell you," he said, smiling.

Talbot theorized that some second-place finishers' problems the following season stem, at least in part, from the aftershocks of a go-for-broke approach that made reaching the final possible.

"Some teams would make [short-term personnel moves], sacrifice a couple of young guys to get some better players, then the next year, lose those guys," Talbot said.

The Penguins, it should be noted, made such a deal in February, sending Colby Armstrong, Erik Christensen, Angelo Esposito and a first-round draft choice to Atlanta for Marian Hossa.

While it's difficult to deal with losing in the final, whatever the reason, runners-up tend to fare considerably worse in the season that follows.

Since 1996, when Colorado swept Florida in the championship series, only one Cup loser – the 1999-2000 Dallas Stars – managed to win a single playoff series the following year. Four of the 11 didn't even qualify for the playoffs.

Penguins defenseman Sergei Gonchar played on one of those teams, the 1998 Washington Capitals. They went from losing to Detroit in the final to a 31-45-6 record the following season.

"It seems like you're pretty much playing or working out for two years," Gonchar said. "Sometimes, you can lose your focus. It seems like there is so much hockey, so much travel."

And that's without a trip across the Atlantic, like the one the Penguins began last evening, when they left for Sweden.

Going to Stockholm figures to create a unique set of problems for the Penguins, but even a standard-issue schedule can grind down a club coming off a long season and short summer.

The challenge of winning a Cup 12 months after losing in the final has been further complicated in recent years by liberalized free agency. That also explains why no champion has repeated since Detroit in 1997 and 1998.

"Obviously, there's a lot of player movement now," defenseman Brooks Orpik said. "When you have [successful] teams, guys are targeted by other teams and it's tough to keep guys together."

The Penguins were able to re-sign Orpik during the off-season, but are trying to compensate for the loss of key contributors like Hossa and Ryan Malone. At the same time, many of the clubs with which they compete have upgraded their personnel.

Players' reactions to learning of the struggles Cup runners-up had the next season ranged from mild amusement to genuine surprise to professional curiosity.

Far more uniform was their insistence that the Penguins are a viable threat to end the second-place slump.

"I don't [care] about it," Talbot said, "because I know we can win."

It seems a nearly impossible challenge in this day and age to return from losing the Cup to hoisting it 12 months later. If any team could prepare for the challenge, however, it was the Penguins. Returning a top-tier core of players from 2008, there was little doubt that Pittsburgh would at the very least have a long run in the 2009 playoffs.

Having so many youthful players in key roles and being, in general, well-conditioned should work in their favor. But even if their bodies hold up, keeping a sharp psychological edge during the dog days of winter might be tough.

"I don't think that physically, it will be a test," Crosby said. "But mentally, it will be a test, for sure."

Not necessarily are they are doomed to fail. Especially if they take their cue from teammates like Crosby, whose passion for his work might be his most underrated asset. "I know Sid won't be sick of hockey at any point in the year," Orpik said, laughing. "I don't know about other guys."

He has a point, but he also seems confident the relaxed atmosphere in the Penguins' locker room, a carryover from last season, could have benefits as the season moves along. "It's a fun group to be around," Orpik said. "When you hit those stretches in the middle of the season where you're kind of plugging away, we have a group that kind of picks you up and pushes you through with the energy we have in here."

They'll need that, if they're to be a factor in the 2009 playoffs. They'll need to find satisfactory replacements for guys like Hossa, Malone, Jarkko Ruutu and Georges Laraque, too. To stay healthy. To be lucky.

"We know it's not going to be easy," general manager Ray Shero said. "We've talked about that, and the players understand that, too. We've got to make the playoffs, become a competitive team and find our identity. "We go through that every year. Hopefully, we'll be the team that breaks that streak." ■

Of course, it's not just the players who are hungry for a winner. Buoyed by the Steelers' success this decade, Pittsburgh fans had their appetites for the Stanley Cup whetted with the finals appearance in 2008. This year, they were ready to see their team return to the Promised Land.

October

Fleury almost saves
HOME OPENER

October 11, 2008 • By Dave Molinari

Goalie Marc-Andre Fleury was named the No. 1 star of the game for his work in the Penguins' 2-1 overtime loss to New Jersey at Mellon Arena. He deserved more, though. Two points instead of one, at the very least.

Or, even better, a written apology from his teammates for the way they performed in front of him. "If he's not there, it would [have been] a horrible game," winger Pascal Dupuis said. "They played a way better game than we did. You get beat, one on one all over the ice, you're not going to win many games."

That's a reasonable assessment.

The Devils ran up a 49-15 advantage in shots, including a 39-7 margin after the opening period. New Jersey didn't look much like a team that had traveled after playing the previous night, while the Penguins looked a lot like a group that had played in Sweden a week before. Then been forced to swim home.

"We didn't work," coach Michel Therrien said.

"It's pretty simple."

Even so, Fleury kept his team in contention for a victory until there were 37.6 seconds left in overtime, when Zach Parise of the Devils beat him with a wrist shot from the left dot for the winner.

"Without Marc, we don't even get a point," center Sidney Crosby said.

"We didn't deserve it. It's funny how it works that way. We didn't do what it takes to win that game."

Still, Fleury seemed poised to make Miroslav Satan's power-play goal at 11:52 of the opening period – Satan's first goal as a Penguins player – stand up as the winner until the Devils tied it on a fluke goal at 17:31 of the third.

That's when a Patrik Elias centering pass from the left-wing boards hit the right skate of Penguins defenseman Hal Gill, who said he was "trying to play in the middle" of two Devils stationed in front of the net, and sailed behind Fleury.

"That's a tough goal to allow," Fleury said. "But it happens sometimes."

The Penguins (1-1-1) dressed seven defensemen although one of them, Darryl Sydor, played left wing alongside Mike Zigomanis and Eric Godard on the fourth line. Bill Thomas and Paul Bissonnette, wingers who usually play on that unit, were healthy scratches.

Therrien said he deployed Sydor, who presumably would have been scratched otherwise, up front "because we wanted to use him on the second unit of the power play."

Sydor said he never had played a full game on the wing since breaking into the NHL in the 1991-92 season, and clearly did not endorse, let alone request, the move. Even so, he declined to make a public issue of it.

"I'll keep my thoughts to myself and just be professional," he said.

Sydor was not on the ice when Satan swiped a

loose puck past Devils goalie Martin Brodeur from the right side of the crease 24 seconds after the first of the Penguins' four power plays began.

The power play hardly qualified as menacing, but its showing was significantly better than last weekend, when it went 1 for 14 against the Senators.

"Obviously, it was an improvement from the last couple games," Crosby said.

There's every reason to suspect the Penguins' sluggish performance was a by-product of their trip to Europe but, to a man, they downplayed the impact of opening the season in Stockholm.

Exhibit A: Their strong work in the first 20 minutes, when they had an advantage in play much of the time, and did no worse than break even for most of the rest. "You can start looking for excuses, but we were fine in the first period," forward Matt Cooke said. "We just got away from our game."

Kind of hard to argue with his logic when, after running up a 15-4 edge in shots in the second period, the Devils offered a 20-2 encore in the third. If not for Fleury, New Jersey's margin of victory might have been enormous.

"He played unbelievable," Cooke said. "Made some huge saves. It's just unfortunate that we couldn't get the job done."

Or do much of anything well, for that matter. ▪

October 2008 Results

Penguins vs Senators	W	4-3 OT
Penguins vs. Senators	L	1-3
Penguins vs. Devils	O	1-2 OT
Penguins vs. Flyers	W	3-2 OT
Penguins vs. Capitals	L	3-4
Penguins vs. Maple Leafs	W	4-1
Penguins vs. Bruins	W	2-1 SO
Penguins vs. Hurricanes	W	4-1
Penguins vs. Rangers	O	2-3 O
Penguins vs. Sharks	L	1-2
Penguins vs. Coyotes	L	1-4

To a man, every player who has put on a Penguins sweater has contributed to their success. Though the big names like Malkin and Crosby may get the headlines, hockey is more than any other sport a team game where every player must play his role. Few teams have done this better than the Penguins.

Ring the alarm...
MAYBE

October 17, 2008 • By Bob Smizik

All those alarmists – the ones who were screaming about the inadequacies of the Penguins and demanding change – well, it looks like they might have a point.

All those cool, composed people who were preaching patience and pointing out the season was young and the team still had an outstanding level of talent, well, you know what they say about those who keep their heads while all those around them are losing theirs: They don't understand the situation.

The situation is not dire. It is early, five games into an 82-game season. But nor is the play of the Penguins to be casually dismissed.

There is reason to be concerned.

They blew a three-goal lead at Mellon Arena to lose to the Washington Capitals, 4-3.

The Capitals were supposed to be what the Penguins needed. They have long been a punching bag for the Penguins. It was hoped they'd be the antidote for all that ailed the team. And for the better part of two periods, the Capitals proved to be just that. The Penguins led, 2-0, after one period and 3-0 late in the second.

No one thought much of it when the Capitals' Tomas Fleischmann scored with about five minutes remaining in the second period. But the momentum of the game was changing. When Alexander Semin scored early in the third period, it was time to worry. But the Penguins still looked good on their home ice and with Marc-Andre Fleury in net. No one expected the Washington onslaught that was soon to come.

The Capitals scored two more times in the third period – goals by Michael Nylander and Boyd Gordon – and sent the Penguins to a stunning defeat in front of a sellout crowd that could scarcely believe what it was seeing. "Unacceptable," said a seething coach Michel Therrien of the team's effort in the final 20 minutes.

"We lost because we stopped working in the third period."

Maybe the Penguins thought they were playing the old Capitals, the team they had so long dominated – going 10-1-1 against them in the previous 12 games – and not the young, skilled unit that has been drawing praise from all over the league.

Even Sidney Crosby gave the Capitals a nod. "They have a deep team, a lot of skill, a lot of guys who can beat you. They've really established themselves as a hard-working team, a competitive team. We have a similar look, with some young guys who have done well early on."

They had all that and more as they took the game

to the Penguins and left them embarrassed and beaten in a shocking third period.

What was alarming about the defeat was that the Capitals didn't get a point from Alex Ovechkin, the best goal-scorer in the NHL. Ovechkin got five shots on goal, only two in the first two periods.

What was even more alarming was that the Penguins collapsed in the third period, being outshot, 21-6, and that after dominating the Capitals in the first two periods, outshooting them, 20-9.

What was most alarming was a statistic pointed out by Therrien. "This is the fourth game in a row we haven't scored a goal five-on-five. They're not paying the price to score goals."

Actually, the Penguins have scored one five-on-five goal in the past four games, but that's not much to brag about, and Therrien's point remains on the mark.

The major positive to come out of the game was the team's work on the power play. All three of their goals came that way, with the third coming when they had a two-man advantage.

Crosby might have won the matchup of the NHL's two best offensive players against Ovechkin, but it was scant consolation. He contributed two assists but remains without a goal for the season.

It has to be of some concern that Crosby hasn't scored a goal. But the good side of that problem is he's going to score. Sidney Crosby hasn't forgotten how to score goals.

Five NHL games are not the equivalent of one NFL game. No one of sound judgment would be predicting a dire fate for the Steelers late in the fourth quarter of their first game and no one should be doing the same thing about the Penguins.

Clearly, though, there is work to be done. ■

Nothing comes easy in the NHL, even for stars like Sidney Crosby. There are bumps and bruises along the way – both figuratively and literally – and every team has some off nights. Luckily, those nights were few and far between for the Penguins as the 2008-09 season wore on.

November

A hard lesson to LEARN

November 6, 2008 • By Dave Molinari

This could have – no, should have – been a night for the Penguins to celebrate. To relish a victory that was devoid of suspense. To enjoy a revival of their offense. To savor getting big-time contributions from players counted on to provide them.

Instead, they flirted with one of the most stunning collapses in franchise history, allowing a five-goal lead with less than 22 minutes left in regulation to melt away almost entirely before holding on – barely – for a 5-4 against Edmonton at Mellon Arena.

The two points weren't secure until goalie Marc-Andre Fleury withstood a last-second surge by the Oilers, who sent a puck and center Shawn Horcoff to the net as time was expiring.

More than a few of the Penguins noted, quite correctly, that what matters most is that they got the victory, which raised their record to 7-4-2. Nonetheless, after spending much of the first month of the season squandering third-period leads, the Penguins showed last night that they have nearly perfected the concept.

"I don't know what's going on," Fleury said. "The guys work so hard to get the lead, and the other guys just catch up [with] us."

A game that seemed ready to dissolve into a laugher after Miroslav Satan and Petr Sykora, both former Oilers, got two goals each and Max Talbot scored one to give the Penguins a five-goal cushion nearly morphed into one of the most scalding defeats the Penguins have suffered.

"I think we just got too comfortable," Satan said.

"You can't do that."

Oh, but they can. And do. A lot. The Penguins, you see, embrace late-game leads like they've been coated with weapons-grade anthrax.

"It has to be addressed, but we have to go out there and do it," center Sidney Crosby said. "We can't [just] talk about it."

Didn't seem like there'd be much need for any such disturbing discussions for most of the first two periods.

Satan secured a place on the Penguins' highlights DVD – and, it turns out, put the Penguins in front to stay – with a goal at 9:14 of the opening period.

He was positioned at the right side of the crease and, after a Brooks Orpik shot caromed off the backboards, steered the rebound between his legs. Satan's stick followed a split-second later and he tossed a shot that bounced off the leg pads of goalie Mathieu Garon and over the goal line.

"It was just a reaction," Satan said. "I don't think there was any quicker way to shoot the puck."

Talbot swatted in a Crosby rebound for a short-handed goal at 15:58 and Satan seemed to put the game out of reach at 7:05 of the second when, with two delayed penalties pending against Edmonton, he set up at the left side of the crease and deflected in an Evgeni Malkin slap shot.

Malkin also figured prominently in the fourth goal, controlling a draw against Sam Gagner – he actually pushed the puck behind Gagner – and flipping the puck

into the slot, where Sykora rapped it past Garon at 11:24.

Sykora then drove Garon from the game by chipping in a rebound from the left side of the crease during a power play at 13:03.

At that point, the only question seemed to be whether the Penguins' goal total would reach double figures.

"The first half of the game, we were playing a great hockey game," coach Michel Therrien said.

But Fernando Pisani spoiled Fleury's shutout bid at 18:33 and, more important, triggered a surge that spilled over into the third period.

Tom Gilbert made it 5-2 when his shot from above the right dot bounced off defenseman Rob Scuderi and past Fleury at 2:57 and 28 seconds later, Ales Hemsky got Edmonton within two on a superb individual effort. He poked the puck away from Scuderi near the Penguins' blue line, chased it toward the net and, as it got to the goal line, slid a shot inside the far post with one hand on his stick. The Penguins had a chance to regain their equilibrium during a five-on-three power play that lasted a full two minutes, but were unable to manufacture a goal. And didn't have to wait long to pay for it.

Sheldon Souray exited the penalty box at 8:52 after serving a roughing minor and, seven seconds later, tossed a backhander past Fleury on a breakaway to make it 5-4. Edmonton couldn't generate another goal, and the Penguins were spared what potentially could have been an epic defeat. At least for one more night. ■

November 2008 Results

Penguins vs. Blues	W	6-3
Penguins vs. Oilers	W	5-4
Penguins vs. Islanders	W	4-3 SO
Penguins vs. Red Wings	W	7-6 OT
Penguins vs. Flyers	W	5-4 SO
Penguins vs. Sabres	W	5-2
Penguins vs Wild	L	1-2 SO
Penguins vs. Thrashers	W	3-2
Penguins vs. Canucks	L	1-3
Penguins vs. Islanders	W	5-3
Penguins vs. Sabres	L	3-4
Penguins vs. Devils	W	4-1

Sidney Crosby has become used to seeing the hats fly at Mellon Arena over his four years in the NHL. Though there have been many memorable hat tricks for him already, perhaps the best of 2008–09 was Game 2 of the playoffs against Washington, where Crosby and Alex Ovechkin matched each other goal-for-goal-for-goal.

Shifting gears leads to **STAAL**

November 11, 2008 • By Dave Molinari

Jordan Staal's scorecard

Shifts	29
Time on ice	19:47
Shots on goal	5
Goals	3
Assists	1
Plus/minus	+4

The Penguins expect a lot from Jordan Staal, and they should, when a guy is that big and that strong and has that kind of pedigree.

But they couldn't reasonably expect anything like what Staal gave them during the final 15 or so minutes of their 7-6 overtime victory against Detroit at Joe Louis Arena.

Not from Staal. Not from Sidney Crosby. Not from Mario Lemieux or Bobby Orr or anyone else, for that matter.

Staal scored their final three goals in regulation, then singlehandledly set up Ruslan Fedotenko's winner at 3:49 of overtime by stealing the puck from Pavel Datsyuk, one of the Red Wings' all-world forwards. "You can't step up much more than that," Crosby said. No, probably not. Not unless your only weakness is rooted in a Kryptonite allergy.

"It seemed like everything I touched went in the back of the net," Staal said. "I'll take it." A lot of the pucks he has touched lately have turned up there. Staal has five goals in the past four games, the kind of rampage he hasn't produced since scoring 29 times as a rookie.

The key now is to show up on the scoresheet regularly to make this a trend.

"It's only one step," he said. "As long as I keep working the way I have been, I'm sure the puck will keep going in."

Staal's hat trick was his second in the NHL and allowed the Penguins (9-4-2) to claim a tiny measure of revenge for their six-game loss to Detroit in the Stanley Cup final in the spring.

"The last time we played them, it wasn't the best," Crosby said.

The Penguins seemed to be in particular trouble at 10:14 of the third.

After Evgeni Malkin and Staal had scored in a span of 72 seconds to pull them within one, Jiri Hudler beat goalie Marc-Andre Fleury from the top of the right circle to restore Detroit's two-goal advantage.

"It's something I'd like to see again," Fleury said. "I don't like to give those up ... I was mad at myself for giving up that goal to cut the momentum and give

them a two-goal lead again."

Turned out to be a minor setback, though, thanks to Staal's outburst.

"He's on top of his game now," coach Michel Therrien said. "That's a good sign for us."

The Penguins won despite a lopsided defeat in special-teams play.

Detroit scored on 3 of 5 power plays, while the Penguins were 1 for 5 with the extra man.

"Our special teams were not too good," Therrien said. "We took some penalties, and they made us pay." Still, the only real loss for the Penguins likely was defenseman Rob Scuderi, who was struck on the outside of his left foot by a Nicklas Lidstrom shot midway through the first period. Scuderi left the game and, after returning early in the second, went back to the locker room and was not seen again.

Crosby gave the Penguins a 1-0 lead at 4:34 of the opening period, but Darren McCarty and Tomas Holmstrom countered for Detroit before the intermission.

Johan Franzen put Detroit up, 3-1, before Max Talbot got a goal for the Penguins, but Datsyuk struck at 18:02 of the second to make it 4-2.

Henrik Zetterberg seemed to put the game out of reach at 5:03 of the third – "It looked pretty tough for us at 5-2, especially against Detroit," Therrien said – but Malkin triggered the Penguins' comeback with a 5-on-3 goal at 6:57, setting the stage for Staal's heroics. The Penguins, of course, got just two points for this victory, the same as they had in each of the three games that preceded it.

Nonetheless, pulling off that kind of comeback against an opponent of such high caliber, has the potential to make a lasting impression on their season.

They didn't play a perfect game -- not even close – but still found a way to manufacture a victory, on the road, against one of the league's elite clubs.

"We just battled back," Therrien said. "We showed a lot of character winning that game." ∎

Blessed with the hands, work ethic, and nose for the game that run in the Staal family, Jordan Staal has played just about every role possible in his short career. Occasionally a third-line checker, Staal can just as quickly turn around and score a hat trick.

Handled with EASE

December 31, 2009 • By Dave Molinari

The Eastern Conference standings put the gap between Boston and the Penguins at 18 points. The Penguins can only hope the actual difference between them isn't even greater.

Boston's 5-2 victory at Mellon Arena was the Bruins' ninth in a row, and raised their record to 28-5-4. And there is nothing even remotely fluky about it. The Bruins are skilled and efficient, confident and opportunistic. They make few mistakes, and are quick to capitalize on any their opponents commit. The Penguins, conversely, have lost three of their past four games overall, and five of their past six on home ice. They are 19-14-4 and are clinging – barely – to seventh place in the conference.

And their prospects for immediate improvement aren't particularly good.

Indeed, the Penguins are troubled enough by how things have gone of late that they convened a players-only meeting immediately after the game.

"I think team attitude is the biggest thing," defenseman Brooks Orpik said. "I don't know if it's poor. I think maybe it's just the approach or lack of preparation going into it.

"These are definitely the times that test the character.

It's easy to be a good teammate when things are going well. I think when things are going rough like they are now, that's when you see each other's true colors.

"You would hope that everyone in the room kind of stays the path and works for a resolution here, but that's easier said than done sometimes."

Coach Michel Therrien said, "it's about time they had a meeting," and added that, "I'm anxious to see what's going to come out of this."

He probably isn't nearly as eager to get another look at the Bruins, who have established themselves as the dominant team in the East.

"They're 20 guys buying into a system and playing for each other," left winger Matt Cooke said. "That's a lesson we can learn from that team.

"It doesn't matter what system is in play. You have to have everyone buy in, and have everyone play to the best of their abilities. They're definitely getting that right now."

Therrien, meanwhile, suggested that some of his players – he didn't identify them – are focused more on individual objectives than those of the group.

"We've got to start thinking about the team concept, not personal agendas," he said. "Let's start from there."

Though the regular season had frustrating moments like the 5-2 home loss to Boston, Marc-Andre Fleury and his teammates made the wins count when they mattered. Boston may have run away to the top record in the conference, but they were the ones sitting at home watching the Penguins hoist the Cup in June.

Although Boston had a 16-10 edge in shots during the first period, the Penguins got the only goal then as Petr Sykora backhanded a Ruslan Fedotenko rebound past Bruins goalie Tim Thomas at 17:00 for his 13th of the season. The second assist went to Dustin Jeffrey, his first point in the NHL.

Boston pulled even on a Zdeno Chara power-play goal at 4:46 of the second and converted on its next man advantage when Marc Savard put in a David Krejci set-up during a 4-on-3 at 9:30.

Pascal Dupuis tied it, 2-2, at 15:13 by lashing a slap shot over Thomas' glove from the top of the left circle for his ninth of the season. The goal was made possible by Sidney Crosby, who plucked a Chara clearing attempt out of the air along the right-wing boards, then put a cross-ice pass on Dupuis' stick.

Just 90 seconds later, however, the Bruins went in front to stay after Evgeni Malkin's pass in the Penguins' end caromed off a skate, triggering a sequence that ended with Blake Kessel steering in a Savard feed from the front lip of the crease.

Martin St. Pierre put the game out of reach with a shorthanded goal at 5:28 of the third, and Dennis Wideman rubbed it in by scoring from above the left circle at 9:38.

"We have a good team, and we know we can do better than we are right now," goalie Marc-Andre Fleury said.

"We have to find a way to win." ∎

December 2008 Results

Penguins vs. Rangers	O	2-3 SO
Penguins vs. Hurricanes	W	5-2
Penguins vs. Senators	L	2-3
Penguins vs. Sabres	L	4-3
Penguins vs. Devils	L	1-4
Penguins vs. Islanders	W	9-2
Penguins vs. Flyers	L	3-6
Penguins vs. Thrashers	W	6-3
Penguins vs. Sabres	W	4-3 OT
Penguins vs. Lightning	L	0-2
Penguins vs. Devils	W	1-0
Penguins vs. Canadiens	L	2-3
Penguins vs. Bruins	L	2-5

After players-only meetings and a coaching change stirred things up for the Penguins in mid-season, Pittsburgh went on a tear through the Eastern Conference, culminating in their impressive playoff run punctuated with a sweep of the Carolina Hurricanes.

Sidney Crosby had been waiting the better part of four weeks to score a goal. In light of that, having to hang on for an extra couple of minutes to confirm that he actually had gotten one – an overtime winner, at that – probably shouldn't have seemed so bad.

But it did.

"It was kind of nerve-wracking," said Crosby, whose goal was his first in 10 games.

Turned out to be kind of worth it, though, because that goal, which came on the deflection of an Evgeni Malkin shot 43 seconds into overtime, gave the Penguins a 4-3 victory against Buffalo at HSBC Arena, their third victory in eight games.

The goal did not become official until a video review determined there was not sufficient evidence to overturn the on-ice ruling that Crosby's stick was not above the crossbar when it touched the puck.

"I guess you could say it was worth the wait," Crosby said. "It would have been nice [to score] earlier, but hopefully, we can build on it."

Certainly, it should be easier for the Penguins to build something meaningful on a victory such as this, when they had to scrap and scratch and battle from behind all game, than it would have been on any of their other games in recent weeks, when any foundation would have been laid on a base of quicksand. "We won this one the right way," said winger Pascal Dupuis, who scored the Penguins' first goal. "We worked hard.

"We needed that kind of win. We needed one of those 'effort wins,' not one of those 'lucky-bounce wins.' "

Although Crosby's goal ended the game, defenseman Alex Goligoski's first two-goal game in the NHL allowed the Penguins to be in position to get the victory. "He's kept getting better and better," coach Michel Therrien said. "I think he's feeling a lot of confidence in this league right now."

Goligoski's power-play score at 11:17 of the third period was particularly important, since it pulled the Penguins into a 3-3 tie and proved to be the final goal by either team in regulation.

It also came on the Penguins' only chance with the extra man; Buffalo, conversely had six, which is why the Penguins were quite content to break even in the special-teams battle.

"At the time, it was a little bit frustrating," Therrien said. "But we did a good job about killing [the penalties]."

Crosby's dramatics and Goligoski's goals largely

overshadowed another productive game for Malkin, who had three assists to run his league-leading points total to 58, 11 more than Crosby, who ranks second. Goalie Marc-Andre Fleury, making his third start since returning from a groin injury, also had a strong showing, stopping 32 of 35 shots.

The game certainly began ominously for him, when a harmless-looking shot by Buffalo's Daniel Paille caromed off Penguins defenseman Philippe Boucher and into the net behind Fleury. That was Buffalo's first, but not only, lead of the game.

In fact, the Penguins never went in front until Crosby's goal was deemed to be legal.

"It's always tough when you're trailing right from the start," Fleury said. "But I knew that if I could make some saves, the guys would score some goals."

That didn't happen until after Ales Kotalik made it 2-0 for the Sabres at 5:23 of the second, but Dupuis converted a Miroslav Satan feed 55 seconds later to revive the Penguins.

After Goligoski tied it with the first of his two at 12:23, Clarke MacArthur converted a Paille rebound during a power play at 15:58 to put the Sabres back in front, 3-2, at the second intermission.

The score stayed that way until Paille was sent off for roughing at 10:35 of the third, giving the Penguins their first chance with the extra man.

"[After] you kill five straight power plays, when you get your chance, you pretty much have to score," Goligoski said.

He did, on a wrist shot from the high slot, and that made it possible for Crosby to give the Penguins two things they desperately needed – two points and an infusion of confidence – with his overtime winner. There was nothing easy about the victory, but that just made it all the more satisfying.

"It was a tough win," Fleury said. "But it was good to get." ■

Sidney Crosby has been the man to turn to when Pittsburgh needs big plays. He has scored more than 30 goals in three of his first four seasons, pouring in an impressive 132 total markers in that time.

Lots of
QUESTIONS

January 20, 2009 • By Dave Molinari

The Penguins will have five days off for the NHL's All-Star break and might need almost all that time to settle on the biggest factor in their 2-1 loss to Carolina at Mellon Arena.

Was it because their power play, which has betrayed them so often this season, again failed to produce in a pressure situation, as the Penguins got nothing but frustration from a four-minute power play as regulation was winding down?

Was it because of Hurricanes goalie Cam Ward, whose performance ran the gamut from brilliant to breathtaking as he stopped 32 of 33 shots?

Or was it because, for much of the evening, the Penguins didn't play with the efficiency and urgency they had in most of the previous four games, even though anyone who bothered looking at the Eastern Conference standings posted in the locker room had to recognize the significance of this game?

"It was an important game," Penguins defenseman Philippe Boucher said. "They stepped up their game, and we didn't."

Which is why the Penguins' two-game winning streak — OK, two-game winning smudge — is over.

Why their record has slipped to 23-21-4. Why they are tied with Florida for ninth place in the East. Winning three of their previous four games had given

the Penguins an infusion of confidence and a bit of momentum, but losing to the Hurricanes likely negated all that.

"It will be good to kind of regroup [during the break]," center Sidney Crosby said.

While many of the Penguins will head to vacation spots for a few days, center Evgeni Malkin and defensemen Kris Letang are off to Montreal for the NHL's All-Star festivities. Crosby will accompany them but won't play because of a knee injury.

Crosby was hit for the first time about 15 seconds into the game, when a shot by Carolina defenseman Tim Gleason caught him on underside of his forearm, sending him to the bench.

Crosby returned in time, however, to help set up the Penguins' only goal. Malkin scored it when he collected a Boucher rebound near the left post and, on his second try, jammed it past Ward on a power play at 2:33. The Penguins subsequently survived a two-man disadvantage that lasted 92 seconds — a kill highlighted by several excellent saves by goalie Marc-Andre Fleury and a faceoff win by defenseman Mark Eaton — and remained in front until Ray Whitney scored on a slap shot from the top of the left circle during a power play at 14:30.

Carolina ran up a 13-1 edge in shots during the first half of the second period, and Eric Staal got the

winner when he steered a Justin Williams feed by Fleury from the right side of the crease at 8:01.

"We lost a battle in front of the net," Penguins coach Michel Therrien said. "It's not about Xs and Os. There are times you have to battle, and we lost that battle and they scored the winning goal."

The Penguins had a few chances to pull even during the third – Letang hit the right post during a power play 35 seconds into the period and Miroslav Satan got off a close-range shot from in front about 6½ minutes later – but failed to to capitalize on them.

Their best opportunity to force overtime came when Gleason got a double-minor for high-sticking Malkin at 15:45, but the Penguins couldn't manufacture the goal they needed.

"That's when you want [the power play] to step up," Boucher said. "It was there for us to tie it, and we didn't come through."

Ward then put an exclamation point on Carolina's second victory in as many nights – a burst that came in the wake of a five-game losing streak – by denying Malkin from the slot with nine seconds to play.

When the Penguins reconvene, their long list of injured players should be a bit shorter. Whether more players will translate to more points remains to be seen.

"We have a lot of injuries," Therrien said. "That's the reality. Hopefully, the break will give us some time for players to get healthy, to put a healthy lineup on the ice." ■

January 2009 Results

Penguins vs. Bruins	L	2-4
Penguins vs. Panthers	L	1-6
Penguins vs. Rangers	L	0-4
Penguins vs. Thrashers	W	3-1
Penguins vs. Predators	L	3-5
Penguins vs. Avalanche	L	3-5
Penguins vs. Flyers	W	4-2
Penguins vs. Capitals	L	3-6
Penguins vs. Ducks	W	3-1
Penguins vs. Rangers	W	3-0
Penguins vs. Hurricanes	L	1-2
Penguins vs. Rangers	W	6-2
Penguins vs. Devils	O	3-4 OT
Penguins vs. Maple Leafs	L	4-5

Naturally, a team can't win every game they play, but this scene of Penguins celebrating while opponents mourn has become far more common than the other way around.

Malkin coming out of his shell in third season

January 1, 2009 • By Shelly Anderson

While his teammates sat at their stalls and stared blankly following a players-only meeting in the wake of the stinging 5-2 loss to Boston earlier in the week, Penguins center Evgeni Malkin slipped out of the locker room.

Normally a crooked, chipped-tooth grin waiting to happen, Malkin had his head down and ran a hand over his dark hair as he ducked into the shower area to avoid the advancing media throng and the cameras that unnerve him.

It had been a rare off night for the NHL's leading scorer, no points despite four shots on goal, on the ice for two Bruins goals and a couple trips to the penalty box.

Still, in a Penguins season that has been somewhat disappointing as it nears the halfway point following a run to the Stanley Cup final in June, Malkin is finding life to be good.

It's not that he doesn't care about the team's results — anyone who watches him can see he hates losing as much as his teammates do — but he enjoys the comfort that comes with settling into new surroundings, including a new house and a hockey career that has him on top of the world and almost assuredly headed to his second consecutive All-Star Game.

"Every year is little better," Malkin, 22, said in a thick Russian accent.

In his third NHL season, Malkin is still the tall, shy, good-natured hockey player who arrived in Pittsburgh in August 2006 for his rookie season after an emotional, arduous journey from Magnitogorsk, Russia. He had broken his Russian Super League contract, which he said he signed under duress, and snuck away from his Metallurg team during a trip to Helsinki, Finland.

As his highly promoted and quoted teammate, center Sidney Crosby, has become the face of the NHL, Malkin — known nearly universally now by his nickname "Geno" — quietly has taken some big steps toward independence when he is away from the safety net of the team by learning English better and becoming self-sufficient socially.

That meant moving out of the home of teammate and fellow Russian Sergei Gonchar into his own house recently.

"Big house," Malkin said, adding that he still wants to surround himself with familiar faces, so his Russian girlfriend, Oksana, will be staying with him, and his parents will make extended visits, including one that will start later this month.

He's enjoying the life of a homeowner, or at least most of it.

"I feel OK. I cook," he said. He grills steak and chicken, makes spaghetti and salad. He grocery shops and likes the organic selections at Whole Foods. Who cleans up?

"My girlfriend. Not me," Malkin said. "My mom when she comes."

On the days of home games, he prefers a midday home-prepared steak and salad to going out, and he sticks to the same pregame snack at the rink – he is a jam fiend, slapping it on buttered toast.

"Strawberry, raspberry," he said. "I like it. It's sweet."

Without Gonchar, who had shoulder surgery in October and out for several more weeks, Malkin has had to get by without his go-to Russian ally. He doesn't lean too heavily on Petr Sykora and Ruslan Fedotenko – his linemates recently – who speak Russian. "It's OK. It's my third year. I'm comfortable," said Malkin, who before this season always asked for an interpreter for interviews. He still tends to freeze when the cameras are on, though, and often makes himself scarce when reporters are around.

On charter flights with the team, Malkin has taken to playing cards with English-speaking teammates Matt Cooke, Brooks Orpik, and his road roommate, Mark Eaton. They used to play hearts but now have gotten hooked on another trick-based game, snarples.

"I like it," Malkin said. "It helps me talk [with team-mates]. It's fun."

Who wins?

"Me. Every time. I'm smart," Malkin said, flashing that grin.

Cooke wouldn't quite back that up.

"He wasn't that good at the beginning of the season,

but he's learning," he said. "He's good at counting cards."

On the ice, Malkin is filling out the potential the Penguins saw when they selected him second overall in the 2004 NHL draft.

Malkin, 6 feet 3 and 195 pounds, has 15 goals, 44 assists for 59 points in 37 games going into a rematch with the Bruins in Boston. With slick moves and strong play in both the offensive and defensive ends of the ice, he can dominate games.

When fan voting for the Jan. 25 All-Star Game ends, Malkin is nearly a lock to be a starter for the Eastern Conference. Crosby and Malkin have been 1-2 in ballot-ing for weeks, each with more than a million votes.

"Million?" Malkin said, his eyes widening. "Thank you. I think Pittsburgh fans love hockey so much. They're good fans."

The debate has raged for months, and could con-tinue for years, over whether Malkin, Crosby, 21, or Washington Capitals winger Alex Ovechkin, 23, is the best hockey player in the world. Crosby won the scor-ing title two seasons ago. Ovechkin won it last season, with Malkin the runner-up.

"My favorite is Sid," Malkin said. "Good skater. Good puck control. Good passes. Everything."

Crosby is second in the league to Malkin this sea-son with 50 points.

"More points is maybe because of me better luck," Malkin said. "Sid play better."

Crosby can have all the marketing and media attention, too.

"Sid is good at talking English and talking with media," Malkin said. "I just play hockey." ■

February

REVIVED

February 4, 2009 • By Dave Molinari

He did not, Evgeni Malkin said, feel responsibility for saving this game, let alone the Penguins' season. It just ended up looking that way.

Malkin spearheaded the Penguins' third-period comeback from a 3-0 deficit, then knocked in the winning goal with 15.5 seconds left in overtime of their 4-3 victory against Tampa Bay at Mellon Arena. "He was dominant in every aspect," defenseman Mark Eaton said. "He was first on pucks, physical, making plays. Phenomenal."

Malkin picked a good time to produce his best effort in what has been a pretty good season for him. The victory not only ended their 0-2-1 skid, raised their record to 25-23-5 and hoisted them into a tie for ninth place in the Eastern Conference, but might have provided the impetus for a surge that could carry them into the Stanley Cup playoffs.

Scoring three times in the final 18 minutes of regulation and getting Malkin's winning goal seemed to give them the kind of emotional boost they haven't had in months.

"Hopefully, a period like that can give us the confidence and momentum we need to put a streak together," Eaton said.

Having a productive power play would greatly enhance the chances of that. After squandering their first six chances with the extra man last night, the Penguins capitalized on their seventh to put the game into overtime.

That last power play was made possible when winger Matt Cooke — a marked man in Tampa since a hit on Vincent Lecavalier late last season led to Lecavalier having shoulder surgery — drew a roughing minor from Lightning winger Gary Roberts at the end of a scuffle at 14:53 of the third period.

"I just stopped and put my shoulder in his chest and he punched me in the side of the head," Cooke said. "At that point in the game, I'm not going to do anything back."

His revenge came in the form of a goal by Petr Sykora at 16:31 that completed the Penguins' rally from the 3-0 lead they spotted Tampa Bay in the first two periods.

The Lightning, losers of three consecutive games, outshot the Penguins, 14-5, in the opening period and got the only goal during those 20 minutes.

Two former Penguins, Ryan Malone and Mark Recchi, teamed up to score it at 15:25, as Malone punched in a Recchi rebound after the Penguins failed to clear the puck from in front of their net.

Martin St. Louis made it 2-0 five minutes into the second period, and the Penguins generated just five shots on goalie Mike McKenna during a subsequent two-man advantage that lasted two minutes.

And when Lecavalier scored from below the right

When the Penguins needed a lift in February, it was Evgeni Malkin who stood up to lead his team to a victory. His game-winner against the Tampa Bay Lightning sparked the Penguins out of a funk and lifted them closer to the playoff position they so coveted.

circle at 16:52 of the second to make it 3-0, the Penguins barely registered a pulse.

Malkin revived them with a goal at 2:35 of the third, however, as he swept in a Pascal Dupuis rebound from the crease, and they got another one at 14:06, when defenseman Mark Eaton threw the puck toward the Tampa Bay net from inside the left circle and it caromed off the right skate of Lightning defenseman Steve Eminger and behind McKenna.

"We've been talking about just throwing pucks at the net," Eaton said. "That's what I did. I knew the guy was in the shooting lane to the net side, so I just tried to put it toward the middle and I got lucky."

Sykora tied it on a power play at 16:31, as he was the last Penguin to touch the puck before Tampa Bay defenseman Paul Ranger knocked it over the goal line. That gave him 20 or more goals in 10 consecutive seasons.

"That's something I'm proud of," he said. And Malkin felt the same way about his, especially since it came in such a critical game.

"It's a great game and I feel great," Malkin said. "I think it's a nice game by me."

None of his teammates argued the point.

"He really took the game over," coach Michel Therrien said. "This is what you expect from your best players at crucial times. You could see the fire was in his eyes.

"He was ready to do everything in his power to try and win this hockey game."

It worked. ▧

February 2009 Results

Penguins vs. Canadiens	L	2-4
Penguins vs. Lightning	W	4-3 OT
Penguins vs. Blue Jackets	W	4-1
Penguins vs. Red Wings	L	0-3
Penguins vs. Sharks	W	2-1 SO
Penguins vs. Maple Leafs	L	6-2
Penguins vs. Islanders	O	2-3 SO
Penguins vs. Canadiens	W	5-4
Penguins vs. Flyers	W	5-4
Penguins vs. Capitals	L	5-2
Penguins vs. Islanders	W	1-0
Penguins vs. Blackhawks	W	5-4 OT

When it matters the most, the Penguins seem to always have their best game ready. Sometimes, however, it just requires a forward taking over the game or a goalie making a big breakaway save to ice a win that may not have come otherwise.

So here's your big move, your bold gambit, your urgent deadline deal, perhaps even your last best drastic alteration the wobbly march of the 2008-09 Penguins.

Waiting on a huge trade?

Here it is:

Head coach Michel Therrien dealt into Penguins history for Dan Bylsma, the day before the hockey coach of your Baby Penguins.

Months in the rumor stage, Penguins general manager Ray Shero finally pulled the trigger on this one with the hangover from the Penguins' desultory 6-2 loss in Toronto the night before still buzzing around his skull. That probably means that Therrien, who shepherded this team to within a couple of wins of the franchise's third Stanley Cup just eight months ago, would still be the coach this morning had the Penguins found a way to protect a multi-goal lead in the latter stages of the second period Saturday night against the Maple Leafs.

Watching them allow six consecutive Toronto goals instead was apparently more than Shero could take.

"It wasn't so much the outcome as the way the game was played," Shero insisted. "It's not always so much the score. It's just the direction we were going."

I asked Shero point blank if a player or players came to him with the suggestion that the club could execute a quick U-turn if only Therrien weren't at the wheel, even if reports that the Penguins' locker room has devolved into factions could not be confirmed.

"Absolutely not," said the GM. "Never happened." That's good to hear. That's grand. Especially since Therrien didn't deserve this. Especially since I'd hate to see him disposed of via the long-standing Penguins tradition whereby the players run off the coach regardless of competence or pedigree.

That would be just too Pittsburgh, wouldn't it? It's an igloo tradition that the Penguins barely tolerate the coach in the best of circumstances.

Bob Johnson got grudging respect at best until people started skating around with Lord Stanley's bling over their heads, and Scotty Bowman, only the greatest hockey coach who ever lived, was essentially hounded away from practice.

Shero knows as well as anyone the treacherous politics of NHL hierarchy. His father, Fred, won 390 games and two Stanley Cups in 10 seasons coaching the Philadelphia Flyers and the New York Rangers, and once said famously, "Athletes don't like to think. You use distractions and surprise to hold their interest."

How interested the Penguins become in showing up for the postseason in the way they've failed to show up to this point will perhaps be on display this afternoon on

Long Island, where Dan Bylsma's team takes on the perfectly miserable New York Islanders as a potential first step back toward competence.

"This is the big move," Shero said last night. "This organization, from a player personnel standpoint, probably won't change significantly. The coach of this hockey team is going to see where this is going to take us. Dan Bylsma knows our organization and knows our players. I'd rather do it this way at this point [than hire an experienced NHL coach]. The message to the players is that we're all accountable. We talk to the players about their passion for the game, about their work ethic, their accountability. We've got 25 games left in which to make progress and get into the playoffs."

None of the key players in this souring Penguins drama did Therrien any favors, and Shero's "we're all accountable" is a clear indication that he knows he's among them. Faced with the financial defections of Ryan Malone and Marian Hossa from last year's Eastern Conference champions, Shero's replacements for Therrien's offense — Miroslav Satan and Ruslan Fedetenko — have come up almost comically short, especially on critical shifts in critical games. But Shero's culpability pales in comparison to Therrien's players.

Marc-Andre Fleury let him down like few others with his squishy goaltending, and superstars Sidney Crosby and Evgeni Malkin, for all their individual brilliance, have not become the kind of vocal leaders necessary to replace the intangibles brought to this mission by relatively pedestrian and departed talents such as Colby Armstrong and Jarkko Ruutu.

You can posit that this team's energy and motivation are the responsibility of the head coach, and ultimately that's merely undeniable, but Michel Therrien isn't the

first great hockey guy to lose control of the Penguins. "You hear that in pro sports," Shero said. "The coach has lost the team. I don't want to pinpoint that. It was just a feeling that the time was right. Things were just not going the way I wanted them to go."

If Bylsma finds that U-turn lane in a hurry, Shero's big move will be the fulcrum of a new Penguins history.

I wouldn't count on it. ■

After a playing career that ended with the lockout while playing with the Anaheim Ducks, Dan Bylsma was the surprise acquisition for the Penguins around the trade deadline. The young and untested coach was just the breath of fresh air that the Penguins needed to spark their playoff drive.

Evgeni Malkin hunched over in his locker-room stall in the Air Canada Centre. His eyes were buried in the butts of his hands, and the misery seemed to radiate from him. There was a long stretch when Malkin, oblivious to the teammates, staffers and reporters around him, did not move, except to breathe. The paralysis of despair.

About 10 feet to his left, Sidney Crosby, the Penguins' captain, was undergoing his usual postgame interrogation by the media.

Crosby was offering his perspective on how the Penguins managed to allow six unanswered goals to a thoroughly unimposing Toronto opponent in what became a 6-2 defeat, and why such a devastating loss didn't necessarily reduce the rest of the Penguins' season to a 25-game formality.

Earnest as Crosby's words were, they couldn't begin to explain what the Penguins had just gone through.

They didn't have to, though. Malkin's body language said it all.

A confluence of circumstances and events – some unavoidable, others self-inflicted – has the Penguins staring up at an ever-shrinking window of opportunity to contend for one of the eight playoff positions in the Eastern Conference.

One year ago, they were about to go on a surge that would carry them to the Atlantic Division championship, the No. 2 seed in the East, and, eventually, a berth in the Stanley Cup final.

Now they are caught in an undertow of mediocrity that has dragged them toward the bottom of the conference, has led to a coach losing his job, and could cost ownership a few million dollars if the Penguins sit out the postseason.

General manager Ray Shero has until the NHL trade deadline March 4 to adjust his lineup, and interim coach Dan Bylsma, who replaced Michel Therrien a week before, has even less time to get his team on the kind of roll it likely will need to slip past a couple of clubs.

A look at some of the factors that have shaped their season to date:

Personnel changes

Marian Hossa was the Penguins' most prominent loss via free agency last July and, by almost any measure, their most important one.

However, personnel decisions general manager Ray Shero made during the offseason – most rooted in salary-cap considerations – altered the fundamental makeup of the team, removing much of the grit and toughness that had made it such a difficult group against which to play.

Taken individually, each move Shero made is easy to justify and understand.

No, Ryan Malone wasn't worth the seven-year, $31.5 million commitment Tampa Bay made to him. No, it didn't make good fiscal sense to offer more than two-year deals to Jarkko Ruutu and Adam Hall, who accepted three-year contracts from Ottawa and Tampa Bay, respectively. No, investing a seven-figure salary in Gary Roberts, on whom all the hard miles he had traveled were showing, wasn't wise.

But when those players left and Shero couldn't find adequate replacements, the Penguins lost the ability to wear down other teams with physical play.

Free-agent acquisition Matt Cooke can play a hard-nosed game, but guys like Miroslav Satan do not. And when Satan failed to score goals the way the Penguins had hoped, his $3.5 million contract became Shero's biggest mistake of the offseason.

The shortage of grit on this team has been an issue since July, and will continue to be. If Shero doesn't address it before the trade deadline, he surely will try to via trades or free agency this summer.

Chemistry

The 2007-08 Penguins were an extraordinarily close group, and that spawned a synergy that allowed the team to become even greater than the sum of its parts. But there is no guaranteed way to duplicate the magic that can happen when personalities mesh in just the right way. That resulted in players genuinely playing for each other, but probably helped guys like Ryan Whitney, Marc-Andre Fleury, and Kris Letang, who people close to the team identify as Therrien's favorite whipping boys, cope with the heavy-handed treatment.

The 2008-09 Penguins are, as currently constituted, a fairly ordinary team, with an ordinary chemistry. There's nothing toxic about the atmosphere in their locker room, but nothing special, either.

Injuries

The game in Toronto might well go down as the low point of the Penguins' season. That's rather ironic, because it also was the first time all season they had a chance to dress the 20 players of Therrien's choice.

Sergei Gonchar made his 2008-09 debut at the Air Canada Centre, He had missed the previous 56 games while recovering from surgery to repair a dislocated left shoulder.

Consider these other injuries:

• Fleury, outstanding through the first quarter of the season, subsequently sat out a dozen games while recovering from a groin injury.

• Whitney, who has excellent offensive skills, had off-season foot surgery and didn't play until Dec. 23.

• Mike Zigomanis, an early-season acquisition from Phoenix whose faceoff prowess proved to be an exceptional asset, injured his shoulder Dec. 3 and eventually underwent surgery that will prevent him from playing this season.

All told, 18 players have missed a total of 236 man-games because of injuries and illness so far.

Late-game lapses

The Penguins can't be ruled out of the playoff race just yet, partly because of their knack for late-game comebacks. Of their first 28 victories, no fewer than nine came in games in which they trailed going into the third period. Last season, they won just six times when behind at the second intermission.

But some of the astonishing comebacks they've have been offset by their frequent inability to close out games they led after two periods. If the Penguins would have found a way to hold onto points that were well within their grasp, they wouldn't looking up at most of the conference today. ■

They probably do not play ice hockey at the Western Pennsylvania School for the Blind, but if they did, it would probably resemble last night's first period between the Penguins and the New York Islanders.

Passes went vaguely in the direction of people with their backs turned, shots were fanned on, nets that yawned open went repeatedly ignored, the ice, by definition, proved very slippery.

The second period wasn't as crisp.

When this game started, the Penguins were within three hours of next year, because anything other than a win against the wretched Islanders – the same wretched Islanders against whom they'd lost a shootout nine days before to celebrate the arrival of new coach Dan Bylsma – and this team would be, to borrow a phrase from the infrastructure stimulus, shovel ready.

And not in a good way.

It looked briefly as if the weird science that is this Islanders-Penguins chemistry would yield something different, especially when the suspicion arose that the Islanders had given up shots for Lent, or at least had given up shooting the hockey puck. Alas, New York finally slid one into the vicinity of Marc-Andre Fleury with 12:25 left in the first period. The Penguins, by that point, had shot seven times without presenting any evidence that shooting the puck had anything to do with the business of scoring goals.

If the Penguins can't crush the Islanders like a bug on home ice, what chance do they have of returning from an impending five-game road grind featuring four foes with winning records with the postseason still on the table?

None.

Through 40 minutes of scoreless hockey against the worst team in the NHL, the Penguins further demonstrated that being on the power play has no known relation to scoring either. The Penguins appear to run two kinds of power plays: The kind where they don't score and the kind where they don't even shoot.

The Islanders only run the second kind. New York's top scorer, Mark Streit, does not have half the points of Evgeni Malkin. New York's win total was four fewer than any team in the league when the game started. New York did the Penguins the favor of starting the backup goalie, Yann Danis, and still the Penguins showed no particular interest in keeping their season alive, even for another 48 hours.

Sidney Crosby sat this one out with an ouchy groin. Ryan Whitney went home to New England on a personal matter. But it wasn't as simple as no Crosby, no Whitney, no winny.

By the time an equally desultory third period was half over, all this mess lacked was a real signature

moment, a memorable freeze frame that might somehow encapsulate the fecklessness and timidity of two bad hockey teams. Fortunately, Christopher Minard provided one.

Flying down the slot behind the New York defense in a 0-0 game, Minard sized up Danis, flashed mentally through his shot options, and ... (what?!) ... floated a drop pass into traffic.

Minard was not about to disrupt the perfect awfulness of this, a night to disremember.

Someone else was going to have to take on that responsibility, and with only 2:28 remaining in the game, someone finally did.

Using the revolutionary offensive concept sometimes called whipping the puck at the net with the idea that even if it doesn't go in, a nearby teammate might run into a rebound, Sergei Gonchar did exactly that from behind a Malkin screen. The rebound got swept across the line by Petr Sykora, and the Penguins had the only goal in a long night of terrible hockey.

"I thought we had good chances against [Danis],

we just couldn't put it in," said defenseman Brooks Orpik in a less than exuberant dressing room. "As frustrating as it was not getting any goals for the first two periods, not getting any until the final two minutes, I thought we stayed patient.

"I thought we kept our composure pretty well."

Is that what that was, composure?

Smelled like a noxious mix of disinterest and incompetence.

"Most of their shots in the third period came on the power play and it wasn't so much great plays by them," said Islanders coach Scott Gordon. "It was our inability to get the puck down the ice when we had opportunities, and they got chances off of those."

The Penguins can fool themselves to whatever extent they please that they earned two points that were absolutely indispensable last night, but the way they've played the Islanders over the past 125 minutes of ice time plus a shootout has left little doubt that they've kissed this season good-bye. ■

Not every win can be a miraculous exhibition of world-class hockey. In the NHL, some wins must come ugly, but two points are two points. The Penguins proved that with their 1-0 win over the Islanders, locking up the vital points despite suffering an off night.

March

Road trip saves SEASON

March 10, 2009 • By Dave Molinari

The road trip was supposed to make the obvious, official. To put the Penguins' season on mathematical life support, make their eventual elimination from the Eastern Conference playoff race nothing more than a formality.

To make it possible for the Penguins, when they returned home with two, maybe three, points to show for their visits to Chicago, Dallas, Tampa Bay, Florida and Washington, to focus on more pressing concerns. Scheduling mid-April vacations, for example, and evaluating the top-end talent available in the June entry draft.

It all seemed perfectly reasonable for a team that had won two of its previous 12 away games.

Except that the 10-day span that was supposed to sabotage the Penguins' season turned out to be its salvation, as they ran off five consecutive road victories, matching their total between Dec. 18 and Feb. 21.

The Penguins knew going in, of course, that it was possible they would put together the first 5-0 road trip in franchise history. Just as they were aware there was absolutely no reason to expect it.

"I think we were 2-9 or something like that on the road before the trip," defenseman Brooks Orpik said yesterday. "So who would have thought that would have happened?"

Probably no one who doesn't regard hallucinogens as one of the primary food groups.

Nonetheless, the Penguins' improbable surge has lifted them from the periphery of the Eastern playoff pack and placed them in the midst of a group fighting for the final four berths.

Whether they ultimately will claim one of those might hinge on what they can accomplish while playing nine of their next 10 games at Mellon Arena, beginning with one against Florida.

While no one expects them to go 9 for 9 – at least no one who failed to foresee them going 5 for 5 on the road – this extended homestand, which will be interrupted only by a trip Thursday to Columbus, should give them an opportunity to tighten their hold on a playoff spot.

"After a 10-day road trip, it's kind of nice to know that you're home for a while," center Jordan Staal said.

That's understandable, although a case could be made that the Penguins actually will have too many games at home for their own good. Teams sometimes get stale over the course of a prolonged stretch at home, and a few players acknowledged that they'd prefer to

There was perhaps no greater run in the Penguins' regular season that the five-game road swing to kick off March. The team was hitting on all cylinders, winning all five contests and charging into the thick of the playoff race.

have a trip or two simply for variety.

"I like the change sometimes, the change of atmosphere," goalie Marc-Andre Fleury said. "Just to get into a game that's different, I like that."

Most of his teammates, however, insist there is no downside to having so many games at Mellon Arena, where the Penguins have won eight of their past 10 games and are 17-12-2 for the season.

Orpik, smiling broadly, volunteered that "maybe some guys get sick of hearing their wives tell them what to do," but was quick to add that the opportunity to generate points and momentum by winning on home ice outweighs all other considerations.

"You want to develop what we did toward the end of last year, that home-ice advantage," he said. "We were really tough to play against at home. That's something that really helped us in the playoffs."

"We've done a lot of good things, but we still have a ways to go to be the team we can be," Bylsma said. "And we have 15 games to do it."

March 2009 Results

Penguins vs. Stars	W	4-1
Penguins vs. Lightning	W	3-1
Penguins vs. Panthers	W	4-1
Penguins vs. Capitals	W	4-3 SO
Penguins vs. Panthers	W	4-3 SO
Penguins vs. Blue Jackets	O	3-4 SO
Penguins vs. Senators	O	3-4 SO
Penguins vs. Bruins	W	6-4
Penguins vs. Thrashers	W	6-2
Penguins vs. Kings	W	4-1
Penguins vs. Flyers	L	1-3
Penguins vs. Flames	W	2-0
Penguins vs. Rangers	W	4-3

The five-game road winning streak to open March did not guarantee a playoff spot. As Dan Bylsma was quick to point out, Marc-Andre Fleury and the team still had 15 games left to make or break their season.

The book on
DAN BYLSMA

March 25, 2009 • By Gene Collier

The co-author of two books, Penguins coach Dan Bylsma would appear to be hard at work on the completion of an instructional trilogy.

With his father, Jay, Bylsma has written "So Your Son Wants to Play in the NHL" and its sequel, "So You Want to Play in the NHL," and though there is no working title for the subsequent text and "So Your Mother Wants to Play in the NHL" is probably out, there's very likely a prime market for "So Your Underachieving NHL Team Needs a Late-Season Slap in the Psyche."

Publishers haven't lined up yet, but who better to write that one?

Five-and-a-half weeks looks like all the dossier Bylsma needs. It has been only that long since Bylsma swapped nurturing the Baby Penguins for coaching the presumably adult version, which at the time had buried itself well short of expectations, not to mention the playoffs.

But with Bylsma behind the bench, the Penguins suddenly went a month between regulation losses, piled up 27 points in his first 16 games, and jet-packed into the middle of the postseason field.

Could someone at least feign surprise around here? Not yesterday.

"This day and age, it's like the old Yogi-ism, 90 percent of the game is half mental, and a lot of that is true," said Penguins defenseman Mark Eaton after another of Bylsma's upbeat practices. "A month ago this was a pretty fragile hockey team with a timid attitude. Now it's like we feel there's nothing we can't do. We can get behind, come back and win, but it was a long time coming.

"I think everyone knew the team had this kind of potential. Going back to the beginning of the year, we knew this team was capable of playing this kind of hockey."

You'd hate to think that all this team was waiting for was for Michel Therrien to be shoved off the ice floe, in part because that would undervalue what Bylsma's done for this team. Only six first-time coaches in the entire history of the National Hockey League ever started their careers at a higher rate of success. Certainly Bylsma got a huge assist from general manager Ray Shero, perhaps the only man in the building with a hotter hand than he. It was Shero who brought Bill Guerin to town at the trade deadline, alone with Chris Kunitz and Craig Adams, amping the toughness and agitation quotients back to customary levels. But it was Bylsma who had to walk into that room and read the faces. To see where this team was and take it to another place.

"At times before he got here," Sidney Crosby said yesterday, "we could all look around the room and see guys who could give more than they were giving. It

wasn't easy for him. It's been a combination of things, but part of it was we had to face up to the fact that we weren't doing everything we could do."

Perhaps it seems almost unremarkable, what these Penguins have done in 5 ½ weeks, because Bylsma has done it without any verbal slashing or roughing, at least not in public. This isn't anything like Mike Tomlin's new-sheriff-in-town transition, initially derided in a similarly veteran locker room and only slowly and even grudgingly assimilated. Moreover, Bylsma wouldn't even take credit for the sudden shift in Penguins tactics, claiming he was merely explaining Therrien systems in new terms.

"Everyone's buying in," said center Tyler Kennedy. "Everyone's being more accountable. Guys have just been more responsible."

In any event, there's no denying that Shero looks pretty smart as the Penguins prepare to see how they'll bounce back against the Calgary Flames after a rare loss. Bylsma looks even smarter, a notion that the head coach rejected pretty flatly outside his office yesterday. "I can say clearly that I'm not that smart," he said. "The players here have just bought into a different mindset and played a little different tempo. We have good players here who were willing to work at establishing our identity as a hockey team. It's usually something you develop in the first 25 to 30 games and then you hone for the next 20 or 30. Here we've done it all in 17.

"But the credit goes to the players. To be honest, I was not surprised at all that things went that way."

Eight games remain until a postseason that to some seemed impossible only a month ago (guilty), but Bylsma's team must still sense the desperation. "We've got to come back hard tonight," said Guerin.

"We don't want to get too far ahead of ourselves." Maybe this team isn't one you'd necessarily write a book about just yet, but you've got to like the outline. ■

Dan Bylsma's hiring looked like a smart move just 16 games after the fact. With 27 points earned in that span and the team playing loose, quality hockey reminiscent of the previous season, Ray Shero and the front office staff must have been pleased.

Bring on the
FLYERS

April 11, 2009 • By Dave Molinari

The Penguins have made a habit of winning NHL scoring championships during the past couple of decades.

Facing Philadelphia in the Stanley Cup playoffs is starting to become part of their routine, too.

Evgeni Malkin scored their first goal in a 3-1 victory against Montreal at the Bell Centre to secure his first Art Ross Trophy and the franchise's 13th in the past 21 years as the Penguins assured themselves of a first-round matchup with the Flyers, one of their most fierce rivals.

"Two teams that know each other pretty well," Penguins center Sidney Crosby said.

Yeah, and that don't care for each other even a little bit.

The Penguins defeated Philadelphia in five games in the Eastern Conference final last spring.

That series wasn't nearly as competitive as the NHL scoring race, which Malkin finally won with 113 points, three more than Washington left winger Alex Ovechkin.

"It feels great," Malkin said.

Crosby has all but formally clinched third in the scoring race.

He finished with 103 points, while Detroit's Pavel Datsyuk, who is fourth, has 97 going into the Red Wings' final game today in Chicago.

Los Angeles, with three scoring titles by Wayne Gretzky, is the only franchise with more than one during the 21 seasons when the Penguins have won 13. Their domination includes six by Mario Lemieux, five by Jaromir Jagr and one each by Malkin and Crosby. The Penguins (45-28-9) finished with 99 points, the sixth-highest total in franchise history.

This was, not surprisingly, the only one of those 45 victories they earned by virtue of scoring two short-handed goals during the same penalty.

What made that feat all the more remarkable was that until Max Talbot and Kris Letang scored during a 55-second span while Brooks Orpik was serving a cross-checking minor midway through the third period, Canadiens goalie Carey Price had been almost unbeatable.

Aside from a rebound that Malkin backhanded between his legs 69 seconds into the game, Price had turned aside everything the Penguins threw at him. That included a sensational glove save on Matt Cooke at 18:02 of the second period and a superb stop on Bill Guerin from inside the right circle 17.4 seconds before the second intermission.

"He played well," Cooke said. "It certainly wasn't his fault [that Montreal lost]."

Price's counterpart, Marc-Andre Fleury, had a pretty decent night of his own, rejecting 29 of 30 shots. The

The Penguins played their best hockey when it mattered the most, entering their playoff matchup with the Flyers riding the crest of a winning wave. The Penguins had turned an underachieving start into 99 points, the sixth-best total in franchise history.

only one to elude him was a screen shot from the left point by Roman Hamrlik at 17:29 of the opening period.

That was the last goal by either team until 9:46 of the third, when Talbot — who had a short-handed goal in the first period disallowed because he knocked it in with a high stick — converted a Pascal Dupuis set up on what amounted to a two-on-zero break.

Talbot's goal was the last one the Penguins would need, but Letang removed any doubt about the outcome by beating Price from the outer edge of the left circle at 10:41, one second before Orpik was to return.

"We've been doing great killing penalties with the new system," Letang said. "When you see an opportunity, you jump into the play, and that's what happened."

There's something else of note that happened over the past eight weeks: The Penguins went 18-4-3 in the 25 games since Dan Bylsma replaced Michel Therrien as coach.

"They responded and came back from a desperate situation, a dire situation," Bylsma said.

And, in the process, earned the right to start the playoffs with a best-of-seven series that figures to fairly crackle with passion and intensity.

"It's a good rivalry," Talbot said. "And it's going to be a great series." ■

April 2009 Results

Penguins vs. Devils	W	6-1
Penguins vs. Hurricanes	L	2-3 OT
Penguins vs. Panthers	L	2-4
Penguins vs. Lightning	W	6-4
Penguins vs. Islanders	W	6-1
Penguins vs. Canadiens	W	3-1

This scene is a surprise to no one who has followed hockey in Pennsylvania over the last four decades. The Flyers and Penguins have one of the best and fiercest rivalries in the sport, never passing up an opportunity to lay out some big hits or to drop the gloves and settle things — at least for a while.

GONCHAR:
Man for all seasons

April 19, 2009 • By Shelly Anderson

You want to find a long line? One that can test your patience? Go to the Louvre in Paris and wait for your chance to come eye to homely eye with the Mona Lisa.

Sergei Gonchar has.

Away from the spotlight of the NHL, after the intensity of the playoffs and series such as the one his team is engaged with against the rival Philadelphia Flyers, the Penguins defenseman likes to get away. Gonchar loves to travel. He tours Europe mostly, although he usually ends up in New York for the U.S. Open tennis late rounds just before training camp. "I'm just another guy walking through, enjoying myself with my family," he said. "I'm trying to just enjoy it and see as much as I can."

As a tourist overseas, he rarely gets recognized. He likes it that way.

That's apropos because Gonchar, who turned 35 Monday, very easily could be the most underrated defenseman in the NHL, one whose patience is just one of the considerable virtues that has helped him build a stellar 14-year career.

"He brings experience," Penguins interim coach Dan Bylsma said. "You don't have to win the game on one play. You don't have to do it on one power play. There's a calmness to doing things the right way to get things accomplished on the back end with the defensemen and also on the power play."

Although his string of seasons with 50 or more points was halted at eight because of preseason shoulder surgery that limited him to 25 games in the regular season, he stepped seamlessly back into his role as the Penguins' top defenseman and quarterback of the power play.

Going into Game 3 at the Wachovia Center, he has two assists in two wins against the Flyers.

With an uninterrupted campaign next season, Gonchar – who is in his fourth season with the Penguins after 10 spent mostly with Washington – should eclipse 1,000 games (he is at 929, not counting 85 in the playoffs) and 200 goals (he has 191).

Yet he is rarely one of the first names rattled off when star Penguins are listed.

He is certainly not like forwards Max Talbot and Pascal Dupuis, who embrace the role of team goofballs off the ice and get a lot of media attention.

"Yeah, thank God," Gonchar's defense partner, Brooks Orpik, said with a smile and a shake of the head.

"He's a calm guy, a really humble guy. He just comes in, goes about his business. He's not doing stuff to get himself any extra recognition. He's just there to do his job and do it the best he can – which he obviously does well above average."

Along the way, others tend to follow. The alternate captain's influence is like a comforting, invisible cloak. "He brings a different demeanor for sure," team captain

Sidney Crosby said. "You need different personalities. He would probably be looked at as a guy who thinks about things a little bit more and takes everything in and is more of an observer. He's important. He's been around for a long time and he's seen a lot of things." Gonchar would seem to personify the stereotype of a stoic Russian, but beneath that exterior is a big heart. Orpik admires Gonchar's ability to transfer his extensive knowledge of the game.

"He doesn't say much, but when he picks his spots, everyone kind of shuts up and listens because he doesn't speak very much," Orpik said.

A strong example of Gonchar's generosity away from the rink was the way he took star center and fellow Russian Evgeni Malkin under his wing. "My first time here, he helped me," said Malkin, who spoke no English and arrived in August 2006 under difficult circumstances after a bad breakup with his hometown team, Metallurg Magnitogorsk. "He called my agent, called my parents. He supported me."

They remain close.

"He's a smart guy. A great guy," Malkin said. "Maybe a bit quiet, shy, but I think he's a very smart guy."

Gonchar opened his home to Malkin until earlier this season, when Malkin bought a house, and acted as mentor and unofficial interpreter and spokesperson. "I remember how tough it was for myself," Gonchar said of arriving in the United States in 1993.

"I didn't speak any English. Going back to growing up, you're playing for the team and they take care of everything – you live in the dormitory, there's food for you. You have to play hockey and nothing else. [Malkin] had a similar setup in Magnitogorsk. His town was taking care of things for him, plus his parents were there.

"Now your life is changing completely, and you don't know what to do. I remember how tough it was. I just decided it would be the right thing to do, and I guess it worked out well."

Unlike Malkin, who was born in 1986, Gonchar can recall growing up in the Soviet Union, in Chelyabinsk.

He wanted to play soccer, but his father suggested he didn't quite have the speed and pointed him toward hockey. Traktor Chelyabinsk was a renowned hockey program.

When Gonchar was a teenager and playing for his national team, the Soviet Union broke up. It affected him, but not the way you might think.

"We were preparing ourselves for what at that time was the European Cup," he said. "We had a very good team going into it. Then, all of a sudden, the change happened. Now, we have to forget about the teammates from Ukraine, Kazakhstan. They're not there anymore. "As a kid, you don't remember all the politics and stuff."

Gonchar isn't as one-dimensional now. He's a family man – daughter Victoria was born just 7 weeks ago, and he and his wife, Ksenia, have another daughter, Natalie. Besides traveling, he and Ksenia like to go to the theater in Russia.

During the season, though, Gonchar is a homebody.

"He likes to play with [his] kids, with Natalie," Malkin said. "He relaxes and watches tennis." And occasionally coaxes his teammates to expand their horizons.

"He did get me in Montreal to try Russian food, which I was a little nervous about," Orpik said. "Borscht is the beet soup. I hate beets, but the soup is really good.

"I've been three times now when we've been in Montreal."

That's the Gonchar influence. ■

Eastern Conference Quarterfinals

A fabulous FIVE

April 25, 2009 • By Dave Molinari

The Penguins spent much of the week insisting they were capable of playing better than they had been. Then went out and proved it.

Except that for much of the afternoon, it didn't seem to matter.

Roughly 24 minutes into their finest performance of the playoffs, they were down three goals and facing the daunting task of trying to come back in front of 20,072 well-caffeinated fans, most fairly oozing hatred for them.

Seemed like a perfect time to panic.

The Penguins didn't.

And they got a 5-3 victory in Game 6 of their opening-round series against Philadelphia, along with a berth in Round 2 of the Stanley Cup playoffs to show for it.

Their turnaround had an unlikely source – Max Talbot losing a fight to Daniel Carcillo of the Flyers 14 seconds after Philadelphia went up by three – but also was rooted in the Penguins' sheer refusal to stray from their game plan.

"If we had to go back to Pittsburgh [for Game 7], we were going to go back to Pittsburgh," right winger Bill Guerin said. "But we were going to play our game, no matter what. We did, and it worked."

The Penguins had controlled much of the opening period by playing that way, although the Flyers got the only two goals then, and declined to abandon it even as some Philadelphia partisans might have been programming their GPS for a drive across the state to attend the Game 7 that won't happen.

Even when down by a field goal, the Penguins resisted any urge they might have had to alter their style. They kept putting the puck on Flyers goalie Martin Biron – the Penguins finished with a 35-25 edge in shots – and getting it deep in the Philadelphia zone, then keeping it there with their most effective cycling of the series.

This is the second year in the row the Penguins have eliminated the Flyers, likely their most bitter rivals, but Philadelphia competed far more evenly this time, dominating some stretches of the series.

"They were everything we expected," Penguins center Sidney Crosby said. "And maybe more." Crosby, meanwhile, moved the fans who devote so much time and energy to hurling off-color chants at him to silence by scoring into an empty net with 27.3 seconds left in regulation.

It was his second goal of the game, and one that guaranteed the hockey season on the east side of the Commonwealth is over.

Philadelphia captain Mike Richards was able to trip up Sidney Crosby, but he and the rest of his teammates were far from intimidated by the Flyers. They outworked and outhustled their rivals from the east, outshooting them 35-25 and making sure Martin Biron was on his toes all game.

For Marc-Andre Fleury, it was a sweet success to jump right back into playoff hockey and pick up a series win in the Conference Quarterfinals. That the victories came against the hated Flyers was just icing on the cake.

"To get that last one and hear a little bit of silence was definitely gratifying," he said.

There didn't seem to be much chance of a decibel level in single-digits a few hours earlier, after Mike Knuble and Joffrey Lupul scored for the Flyers 51 seconds apart late in the first, and Daniel Briere put them up three at 4:06 of the second.

"We got a 3-0 lead, it should be over," Flyers coach John Stevens said.

Fair point. But, on this day, it was barely getting started.

Immediately after Talbot sacrificed himself in the fight with Carcillo — "Max really stepped up," right winger Tyler Kennedy said. "He showed a ton of guts." — Ruslan Fedotenko converted an Evgeni Malkin rebound, and Mark Eaton knocked a Kennedy rebound out of the air and past Biron at 6:32 to make it 3-2.

"We were just trying to survive after that," Briere said. Didn't work.

Crosby rapped a Guerin rebound out of the air at 16:59 and Sergei Gonchar got the winner on a slap shot at 2:19 of the third as the Penguins rallied from a three-goal deficit to win a playoff game for the third time in franchise history.

"They tested us," interim coach Dan Bylsma said. "That's something we needed to have happen. We've been tested. And we've responded." ∎

Eastern Conference Quarterfinals

Game 1	Penguins 4	Flyers 1
Game 2 (OT)	Penguins 3	Flyers 2
Game 3	Penguins 3	Flyers 6
Game 4	Penguins 3	Flyers 1
Game 5	Penguins 0	Flyers 3
Game 6	Penguins 5	Flyers 3

Rob Scuderi lays out to prevent a pass from reaching Philadelphia's Jeff Carter. After a slow start put them in the hole 3-0, the Penguins defense stepped up to the challenge of the Philadelphia attack.

Orpik's happiness:
PRICELESS

April 28, 2009 • By Ron Cook

If things had worked out a little differently last summer, Brooks Orpik could be playing his hockey at the Staples Center in Los Angeles instead of Mellon Arena. Well, actually, he wouldn't be playing now because the Kings had a lousy season and didn't make the Stanley Cup playoffs. But he could be cashing a bigger check and enjoying that wonderful California weather and kick-back lifestyle.

No thanks, Orpik said.

Give him Pittsburgh any day.

"A guy like [former Penguins teammate] Ryan Malone, if he had to do it all over again, he'd take a lot less to stay here," Orpik said. "I know at the trade deadline, he was begging to come back here.

"A lot of the guys who have left feel that way. The older guys — Gary Roberts, Darryl Sydor, Mark Recchi — used to tell me we have something special here. I think the commitment level — the camaraderie level — that this group of guys has is unique in sports." Orpik grinned, his electric blue eyes dancing even more than usual.

"As stupid and cheesy as that sounds, I really believe it's one of the reasons we are where we are right now."

Where the Penguins are is getting ready for the second round of the playoffs, a year after they made it all the way to the final. The chance to get back and maybe even win the Cup is worth a lot more to Orpik than a few extra dollars in his pay and all of that California cool.

That isn't to say Orpik isn't fabulously compensated with the Penguins. The six-year deal he signed as a free-agent defenseman after last season pays him $3.75 million per year.

The point is Orpik could have grabbed for more, if not from the Kings, then from the New York Rangers, the other team that intrigued him when he was going through the free-agent process. Human nature is to go for as much as you can get. That Orpik didn't doesn't make him any kind of a hero. It just makes him unusual in an era where athletes use their paychecks to keep score among themselves.

"As much as you hate to say it, there are guys who only play for the checks," Orpik said. "If they have to be at practice at 9:15, they show up at 9:15. Then, as soon as practice is over, they're gone.

"That's what I mean when I say it's different here. Guys want to come early and they stay late. The trainers get mad because we stay so long. They have to kick us out so they can go home."

The winning is a big part of it. Sure, it is. Orpik is prominent in that. Going into the games last night, he led all NHL players with 31 hits in the playoffs even if the stats crew in Philadelphia didn't bother crediting him with a single one in Game 3 of the series against the Flyers. He said the number isn't important. What matters is that he feels he's doing something to wear down the opponent over a long series.

"I don't think anyone likes to get hit," Orpik said. "But there are some guys, you can get them off their game. Maybe they don't come through the neutral zone with the same speed. Or maybe they take their eye off the puck and turn it over looking for you instead of worrying about making a play."

Orpik tormented a number of Flyers, especially getting Joffrey Lupul's and Claude Giroux's attention with brutal hits. Those hits didn't get the same airtime on SportsCenter that his four hits during an amazing 15-second sequence against the Detroit Red Wings in Game 3 of the Cup final last season did, but they and his 29 others were a factor in the Penguins advancing in six games. They outhit the notoriously physical Philadelphia bunch, 143-142.

"The stats don't matter to me. What matters to me is what the guys on the other team are thinking," Orpik said.

"You want to go ask them, 'Was that guy fun to play against?' Obviously, you want that answer to be 'no.' "

Flyers center Daniel Briere certainly would say "no" about Orpik. It's fair to think he's one of the guys Orpik took off his game. He got so frustrated with him late in Game 3 that he took a double-minor penalty for high-sticking him, breaking his nose and leaving it gushing blood all over the Wachovia Center ice. Orpik figured it was a small price to pay for Briere's dismay.

"He apologized to me in the handshake line," Orpik said, all but giggling. "If I had more time right then, I would have told him that I expected that from him a lot earlier in the series, as much as I've ran him over the years."

Orpik will renew a lot of acquaintances and maybe even make new friends in the next series.

That much is certain.

So is this: They won't be having nearly as much fun in L.A. ∎

For Brooks Orpik, staying in Pittsburgh and taking a six-year deal was an easy decision. With the advice of current and even former teammates, he was confident in his decision to return to the only professional organization he has ever known.

Just call Talbot "ROCKY"

April 26, 2009 • By Gene Collier

Max Talbot certainly isn't the first guy to be beaten and robbed in South Philadelphia, but he's likely one of the few to be victimized in shifts.

Mike Richards stole a hockey puck from him and fired it at the Penguins' net late in the first period, with Mike Knuble ripping home the rebound to put the Flyers on their way to a 3-0 lead. But it wasn't until early in the second that Talbot was beaten fairly savagely about the face and head by Philadelphia mauler Daniel Carcillo in an incident that would have been a footnote to Game 6 (actually more like a facenote) had not something momentous unfolded in the direct aftermath of the assault.

When Talbot and Carcillo floated to their respective holding cells at 4:21 of the second period, the Penguins were adrift somewhere in 95 minutes and 13 seconds of goal-free offensive hockey.

Fourteen seconds later, Ruslan Fedotenko scored the first of five Penguins goals that turned a frothing Wachovia Center sellout into a wake for a Flyers season that ended in stunningly close proximity to its apex. Coincidence?

Everyone thought not.

"I had to make up for [turning the puck over]," Talbot said in a highly satisfied Penguins dressing room. "That seemed like a good way to do it."

The fight lasted less than a minute, the first 15 seconds being consumed by both parties' inability to get their hands free, but, once that was accomplished, Carcillo landed several hard rights that drove Talbot to the sheet.

"I can see where him fighting might get them going," said Carcillo, who served a one-game suspension earlier in this series for leveling Talbot on a faceoff. "Even him just showing up; it doesn't matter whether you win or lose.

"In hindsight, maybe I shouldn't have fought him." As a noted football coach once said preposterously, "hindsight is 50-50," but this might actually have been the case on the day the Penguins advanced to the Eastern Conference semifinals. They clearly needed more than Max's unsuccessful one-rounder, so there's at least a 50 percent chance it had nothing to do with anything, but higher authorities seemed to agree that this 5-3 Penguins victory might not have come about otherwise.

"When you see what he tried to do, to lift our spirits, it's good when you can follow that up," said Sidney Crosby, who somehow managed to score two goals, generate about 12 good scoring chances, and win 20 of

33 faceoffs without earning a star. "You want good things to happen after something like that."

Even Dan Bylsma, who was spared a possible Game 7 with nearly as many ominous implications as the swine flu, didn't question the significance of this hockey game's one venture into boxing.

"I think Max Talbot really changed the momentum with that," Bylsma said. "Max just took it upon himself. Right after that, we got the goal."

Fedotenko's stuffer merely sliced the Flyers' lead to 3-1, but, when Mark Eaton scored less than two minutes later, any psychological edge the Flyers had established seemed to shift beneath their feet. Eaton came hard to the net on a 3-on-1 the Penguins generated out of Philadelphia's end. Tyler Kennedy shot the puck from the left-wing circle, and Eaton came right up Broad Street on Flyers goalie Martin Biron, slapping the rebound past him with a short baseball swing many a Pirate might envy.

"I was a center fielder [growing up nearby in Delaware], a singles hitter," Eaton laughed. "That was like a bunt down the third base line. I guess baseball came in handy today."

Crosby laughed, too, when asked if he always had suspected he has as good a baseball swing as Eaton, because Crosby's tying goal 10 minutes later came on a similar play. Crosby crashed the net from the wing opposite where Bill Guerin was carrying the puck, and, when Guerin flipped it at Biron, Crosby interrupted Biron's juggling act by swatting the puck behind him in much the same motion.

"I didn't expect to see [Eaton] there doing that, but we'll take 'em any way we can get 'em," said Crosby, who again silenced more than 20,000 tormentors with

customary brilliance. "You've got to go to the net sometimes and you've got to score like that sometimes."

No one would have blamed the Penguins if they had come into Game 6 wondering if they would score again. Biron shut them out in Pittsburgh Thursday night, and though the first period yesterday was rife with scoring chances, they were down, 2-0, at the first intermission and 3-0 at the bell for the Talbot-Carcillo bout.

"Even when we were down, 2-0, 3-0, we kept playing the right way," said Bylsma, now the owner of his first playoff series victory. "They really tested us. In the playoffs, you're going to be challenged. We really got a good punch in the gut from them. They let us know how hard it was going to be."

It was awfully hard until Talbot punched back, and, even though he traded one for about six, he'll take that deal anytime it provides the kind of inspiration with which the Penguins dismissed the Flyers for the second consecutive spring. ∎

Max Talbot may never post the biggest numbers on the score sheet, but he is still invaluable to his team. Tough in the truest sense of the word, he played through a broken foot suffered against Philadelphia in the 2008 playoffs, returning the next year to drop the gloves and ignite his team's push to eliminate the Flyers.

Eastern Conference Semifinals

A KNOCKOUT

May 13, 2009 • By Dave Molinari

The Penguins knocking Washington out of the Stanley Cup playoffs lost its novelty years ago. They have faced the Capitals in the postseason eight times and eliminated them seven.

It has pretty much become a tradition.

But never, ever did the teams play a series like the one that ended with the Penguins' 6-2 victory in Game 7 at the Verizon Center.

It was the most-hyped series in recent NHL history – maybe the most-hyped ever in the second round – and, for six games, it didn't just live up to expectations, it exceeded them. By a lot.

But not in Game 7, as the Penguins seized control in the early minutes and didn't let go until they owned one of the most surprisingly stress-free victories in their playoff history.

"You definitely wouldn't predict a score like this," defenseman Mark Eaton said. "But we'll take it." The Penguins are in the Eastern Conference final for the second year in a row; making them the first team to reach a conference final the year after losing in the Cup final since Detroit did it in 1996.

Defenseman Sergei Gonchar, who missed Games 5 and 6 because of an injury caused by a knee-on-knee hit by Capitals left winger Alex Ovechkin in Game 4 Friday, was back in the Penguins' lineup.

Gonchar wore a brace on his damaged right knee that he said "helped me a lot." He took a fairly regular shift and manned the right point of the power play while logging 15:06 of ice time.

"Obviously, I wasn't 100 percent, but it was Game 7," Gonchar said. "You have to play. I'm sure everyone else would have done it."

Gonchar, who has refused to say whether he believes the hit was dirty, spoke about it with Ovechkin in the handshake line that followed the game. "He said there was no chance he was able to avoid that hit," Gonchar said.

The series had been touted as a showdown between the NHL's two most-celebrated players, Sidney Crosby and Ovechkin, and the Penguins' victory made Crosby a clear winner in the area that mattered most.

On an individual level, however, both dazzled from earliest shifts of Game 1 to the waning minutes of Game 7. Crosby had two goals and an assist last night to finish the series with eight goals and five assists; Ovechkin picked up a goal to end with eight goals and six assists.

"One of the guys said before the game that Sid was born for this," Penguins right winger Bill Guerin said. "As was Ovechkin. Sid just had his good stuff tonight, really stepped up."

Simeon Varlamov, the Capitals' rookie goalie, did

In a battle of the NHL's two biggest stars, it was Sidney Crosby and his Penguins that outshined Alex Ovechkin and his Washington Capitals. The classic series exceeded all expectations, ending in somewhat anticlimactic fashion with the Penguins' 6-2 win in Game 7.

The hockey may not have been better in the opening rounds of the playoffs than in the series against Washington. The seven-game classic had it all: great goals, pumped up fans, and great saves like this one by Marc-Andre Fleury.

that for most of the previous six games, but unraveled in the crucible of Game 7. He allowed four goals on 18 shots before being replaced by veteran Jose Theodore at 2:12 of the second period.

"It wasn't Varlamov's best night," Guerin said. "But the kid played tremendous in the series."

Penguins goalie Marc-Andre Fleury, meanwhile, had a fairly ordinary performance — except for a possible series-saving save on an Ovechkin breakaway three minutes into a scoreless game.

"If that goes in, who knows where the game goes?" Penguins defenseman Brooks Orpik said. "I was thinking to myself right after that, 'Maybe that's the turning point in the game.' It's definitely something you look back on. After that, we kind of dictated the play."

Yeah, kind of.

Crosby put the Penguins in front to stay with a power-play goal at 12:36 of the first, and Craig Adams made it 2-0 eight seconds later. That was the second-fastest two goals in team playoff history; Ron Stackhouse and Rick Kehoe scored seven seconds apart against Boston April 13, 1980. Guerin (28 seconds) and Kris Letang (11:37) drove Varlamov from the game in the second period, and Jordan Staal and Crosby added goals against Theodore as a game that began with high drama morphed into something closer to low-brow comedy.

Not that Game 7 necessarily stripped much of the luster from the series.

"We all knew it was going to be a special series," Gonchar said. "Obviously, the series lived up to expectations. I think everyone's going to remember it." ■

Eastern Conference Semifinals

Game 1	Penguins 2	Capitals 3
Game 2	Penguins 3	Capitals 4
Game 3 (OT)	Penguins 3	Capitals 2
Game 4	Penguins 5	Capitals 3
Game 5 (OT)	Penguins 4	Capitals 3
Game 6 (OT)	Penguins 3	Capitals 5
Game 7	Penguins 6	Capitals 2

Celebrating Penguins goals was a common sight in Game 7 with Washington. Capitals starter Simeon Varlamov was chased from the game, and former Hart Trophy winner Jose Theodore fared little better against a determined Pittsburgh assault.

Crosby wants just one tag

May 17, 2009 • By Ron Cook

There is a difference, Sidney Crosby was saying the other day before he stepped deeper into the Mellon Arena bowels for another tough off-ice workout. It's not so much about being the best hockey player in the world that drives him. "I don't need that tag to sleep at night," he said. It's about being the best hockey player he can be every day, every practice, every game, every shift. "The only time I've ever seen Sid get really [ticked] off is when he feels like he hasn't done everything he's capable of doing," teammate Max Talbot said.

That hasn't been a problem during this Penguins playoff push. Crosby has never played better than he did against the Philadelphia Flyers and Washington Capitals. Although just about everyone long has recognized and admired his all-around brilliance as a two-way player, there has been some criticism that he didn't shoot the puck enough, certainly that he didn't score enough. Well, there Crosby is now, leading the NHL pack in the playoffs with 12 goals, almost all coming after he went hard to the net and paid every bit of the expected physical price.

And that best-player label that the man says is so unimportant in the grand scheme of things?

Clearly, it's his, all his.

That Crosby tormented the Flyers in the first round is no surprise. Philadelphia fans have been chanting obscenities at him since his rookie year when he had the brass to complain to the referees about a high stick to the face from Flyers defenseman Derian Hatcher that was not penalized and left him with a four-stitch cut on his lip and without parts of three teeth. Whiner, those geniuses call him. Crybaby. Soft.

Crosby just laughs and shrugs it all off. "It's been going on for so long that it's just crowd noise now," he said. But don't think for a second that he didn't love doing his part to eliminate the Flyers for the second consecutive spring, including getting two goals in the decisive Game 6 to bring the Penguins back from a 3-0 deficit. "I'm sure Sid takes it personally," Talbot said.

There was extra motivation for Crosby in the Washington series, as well. It wasn't just the silly comments in the fall from Capitals winger Alexander Semin. "What's so special about [Crosby]? I don't see anything special there." It was the talk before and during the series that the Capitals' Great 8 – Alex Ovechkin – was the best player in the world. Maybe that sort of thing doesn't keep Crosby up at night, but he's human, isn't he? He takes great pride in his job, doesn't he? How could that not give him a little extra jump?

Funny, you don't hear much talk now about Ovechkin or, for that matter, Penguins teammate Evgeni Malkin being better than Crosby. Not after Crosby led the Penguins past the Capitals with eight goals. Not after he scored the huge first goal on the road in Game 7 with a fabulous bit of hand-eye coordination, kicking the puck with his right skate to his stick and banging it into the net in a nanosecond. (His ease in doing it was almost unbelievable, actually.) Not after he pilfered the puck from Ovechkin – how cool was that? how appropriate? – and scored the final goal of the series on a breakaway.

"He's our captain, our leader," Penguins goaltender Marc-Andre Fleury said. "The other guys see him flying around the ice on every shift. He's a great example for our team to follow."

"You have no choice but to follow him," Talbot said.

That's not just during the games. It's in those off-ice workouts and at every practice. Crosby is considered a maniacal worker. "All hockey, all the time," Talbot said. "He's always looking for ways to get better." That's why Crosby's response was so predictable in January and February when the Penguins were scuffling just to make the playoffs and some on the outside were questioning his leadership: "When you're losing and things are going bad, you have to work harder," he said. Asked how that is possible for a guy like him who's always working, anyway, he grinned and said, "Oh, you find ways, believe me ... I'll do anything to be successful. I hate not being successful."

You have no idea.

"In practice, you'll miss a pass and he'll give you that look," Talbot said. "He doesn't do it to be mean. He does it because he wants everything to be right."

That's why motivation won't be a problem for Crosby against the Carolina Hurricanes even if he can't draw on outside forces the way he did in the Philadelphia and Washington series.

It would be nice if the Carolina crowd – a lot more docile than the hate-filled Philadelphia fans – would turn nasty toward Crosby. Maybe the Penguins can get the Hurricanes' new No. 1 fan – Bill Cowher – to do something about that. Then again, maybe not. It also would be nice if a Carolina player would be dumb enough to question Crosby's ability or a prominent media type would argue that Hurricanes star Eric Staal is better than Crosby. But neither of those things is likely to happen, either.

No worries.

Crosby still will be amped.

"He's all about this team winning," Penguins defenseman Brooks Orpik said.

You want to know what drives Crosby?

Bingo.

That and being his absolute best, of course. Go ahead, call Crosby the best player in the world, if you like. He'll say thank you, respectful as always, and be quite pleased. Who wouldn't be?

But, really, there's only one tag that Crosby desperately wants.

It's so obvious, isn't it?

Champion.

Stanley Cup champion. ■

Ultimately, it came down to the GOALIES

May 14, 2009 • By Gene Collier

Along 7th Street NW, the young redheaded girl toted her white sack of fast food three hours before Game 7, mounted the first few marble steps of the National Portrait Gallery and sat down to eat 20 feet from where a man was offering professional palm readings.

With palm readings, you should always consult a professional, but the redhead in the VARLAMOV jersey merely munched out, resisting any urge toward pregame mysticism.

Too bad.

Not five hours later, it was evident that had she dragged her red No. 40 shirt just a few steps to her right, she could have been saved some torment. The palm reader might well have taken her hand and seen the whole thing coming.

Don't tell me anyone else did.

Parading right down 7th for this girl and about 20,000 red-shirted Capital fans wedded to the immediate fortunes of Washington goaltending sensation Simeon Varlamov were torment, disappointment, betrayal, pain, bewilderment, bitterness, emptiness, pain, heartache, night sweats, chronic indigestion and pain.

Approximately.

That's what the Penguins can do to you when they play almost perfectly, when they build most of a 5-0 lead in the first hour of the biggest game of the season, when they go gleefully about their traditional spring administration of Capital punishment.

"Probably didn't have his best night," defenseman Brooks Orpik quipped about the Capitals goalie in the somewhat giddy minutes after the Penguins rode a 6-2 spanking into the Eastern Conference final against Boston or Carolina. "But that's hockey for you."

Palm readers, tarot card interpreters and everyday experts among the hockey journalists had long since cast this series as a matchup that would tilt on goaltending, but it tilted to the opposite end of their expectations for most of two weeks, with the rookie Varlamov outplaying playoff-tested Penguins counterpart Marc-Andre Fleury. But in the end, it tilted back violently, and you knew the callow Capitals hero was in trouble at 12:44 of the first period, eight seconds after Sidney Crosby stabilized a pinballing puck near the Washington net and tapped it home for a 1-0 lead. Now, Craig Adams was breaking toward the net with a pass from Ruslan Fedotenko, Adams not having been listed among the top 30 most-frightening offensive puck handlers in this or any other series. But Adams snapped one between Varlamov and the near pipe to put the Penguins up 2-0.

That one had no business getting by Varly, and Varly, though no one knew it at that moment, was quickly, shockingly, going out of business.

Two goals in the first 2:12 of the second period sent him to the bench and brought back to the Capitals goal Jose Theodore, who'd been unceremoniously banished after the first game of this playoff spring. Varlamov had performed pretty much miraculously ever since. The Penguins' third goal, the one Bill Guerin buried just 28 seconds after the first intermission, probably wasn't Varlamov's fault. Washington's Shaone Morrisonn gave Guerin too much room near the top of the left wing circle, and suddenly a series in which 92 percent of the ice time had been played with the score tied or one team having a one-goal lead witnessed its first three-goal lead. Its first four-goal lead and its first five-goal lead were to come.

Not to mention a second five-goal lead.

Through all that, Fleury re-emerged from the margins of severe, hyperventilated criticism to the place he occupied before any of this began — as the superior goaltender. He was never really an issue.

"No, no, why?" said Fedotenko, who had five points in the last five games and scored in three of them. "So many times, he kept us in games. He's been outstanding for us every night"

Fleury's game returned with perfect playoff timing soon after they dropped the puck. He stopped Alexander Ovechkin's wrister, the first serious scoring chance of Game 7, just 1:21 in. But less than two minutes later, the Penguins got all the evidence they needed that this would be Fleury's night, and by extension, certainly theirs.

Ovechkin swept toward him on a breakaway at the end of the third minute, shot high to Fleury's glove side, and the Penguins goalie webbed it with a snapping motion that was one part defiance, nine parts skill. "I never thought Fleury was an issue in this series," coach Dan Bylsma said. "There was a lot of talk about the star players, the power play, the penalty killing, other things that were focused on. He has been fazed by some powerful shots from some very skilled players, but he's made big saves for us in probably every game, and there isn't a player in our room that doesn't think believe he's a big-time goalie for us."

You could almost believe anything about the capabilities of Bylsma's team today. If they can swamp an opponent as good as Washington in the cauldron of a Game 7 road game, what can they not do? ■

What's most important in this picture is what's not in the frame: the puck. At the end of the day, it can be the most technical butterfly, the most graceful stand up kick, or the luckiest flop in the world; and all that matters is that the puck goes in the net.

Eastern Conference Finals

Penguins put final touch on SWEEP

May 26, 2009 • By Dave Molinari

Craig Adams was not part of the Penguins' team that went to the Stanley Cup final a year ago. He didn't experience the pain of their six-game loss to Detroit, the frustration of falling two victories shy of a championship.

Which means Adams might be the perfect guy to offer a clinical assessment of why it really doesn't matter if the Penguins get a chance for revenge against the Red Wings, now that they've locked up a spot in the Cup final by sweeping Carolina in the Eastern Conference final.

"You want to win a Stanley Cup," Adams said, minutes after the Penguins' 4-1 victory against the Hurricanes in Game 4 at the RBC Center. "It doesn't matter if you're playing Detroit or whoever.

"You don't need any extra motivation at this time of year. Obviously, the guys want to beat them, but I don't think they want to beat them more than if it was somebody else."

The Penguins are the first team to return to the Cup final after losing it the previous year since Edmonton did it in 1984, when the Oilers won a rematch with the New York Islanders.

They also are the first team to reach the Cup final in consecutive years with different head coaches since the Penguins of 1991 and '92, who did it with Bob Johnson and Scott Bowman behind their bench. Johnson and Bowman were established — no, legendary — coaches by the time they joined the Penguins. Conversely, Dan Bylsma, who guided them to this final, has been in the NHL for less than 3½ months. But even if he did not touch the Prince of Wales Trophy the Penguins were awarded last night, his fingerprints were all over it.

For when he replaced Michel Therrien in mid-February, the Penguins seemed like a long shot, at best, to get into the playoffs, let alone to be playing for a title. "With the coaching change, we instantly got confidence and started playing the right way," left winger Matt Cooke said.

And they haven't stopped since.

They've gotten some spectacular individual performances along the way — Evgeni Malkin, for example, had nine points in the first three games against Carolina, and Marc-Andre Fleury stopped 30 of 31 shots last night — but playing a solid, responsible team game is what got them this far.

"When you have that much skill and that much tempo, you'd think there'd have to be a down part in the game, but they've been working hard," Carolina forward Scott Walker said. "Defensively, all their guys have been coming back super-hard, and that makes it tough."

Former Conn Smythe Trophy winner Cam Ward was unable to contain the Pittsburgh assault, with no Penguin giving him more fits than Evgeni Malkin. The stellar Russian started the series white-hot, scoring nine points in the first three games.

After a 35-win regular season, Marc-Andre
Fleury stood on his head throughout the
series with Carolina. Other than allowing
four goals in the second game of the series,
he was outstanding, never allowing more
than two goals in the other three games.

Carolina got an early 1-0 lead for the second game in a row — Eric Staal jammed a shot inside the right post at 1:36 of the opening period — but the Penguins never were fazed, and Ruslan Fedotenko steered a Philippe Boucher shot behind Hurricanes goalie Cam Ward at 8:21 to tie the score.

Max Talbot got what proved to be the winning goal at 18:31, when he corralled a loose puck just inside the Penguins' blue line, carried it through the neutral zone and into the Hurricanes' end, then took a shot that Carolina defenseman Anton Babchuk blocked.

Sort of.

Although Babchuk took most of the steam out of Talbot's shot, the puck fluttered through the air and over Ward's glove before dropping into the net to put the Penguins up, 2-1.

"You need a lot of skills and talent to put it top-shelf from the top of the circle with a shot like that," Talbot said, smiling. "All skill."

Bill Guerin delivered the kill shot when he converted a Sidney Crosby set-up at 12:10 of the second, and Crosby fed Adams for an empty-netter with 70 seconds left to close out the scoring. And the series.

And to guarantee the Penguins an encore performance on hockey's greatest stage.

"We know that we've got a special opportunity to go at it again," Crosby said. "And we want to take full advantage of it." ▨

Eastern Conference Finals

Game 1	Penguins 3	Hurricanes 2
Game 2	Penguins 7	Hurricanes 4
Game 3	Penguins 6	Hurricanes 2
Game 4	Penguins 4	Hurricanes 1

The Penguins protected their goalie well in the Eastern Conference finals, and took advantage of a fortuitous bounce off Hurricane defenseman Anton Babchuk to beat Cam Ward. Bill Guerin and Craig Adams provided the icing on the cake, sending a hungry team into a rematch with the Detroit Red Wings.

A surge of
FLOWER POWER

June 6, 2009 • By Robert Dvorchak

In a world where the puck is called the biscuit and an arena is known as the barn, Chris Kunitz dipped into hockey's special vocabulary to describe Marc-Andre Fleury's ability to make impossible saves through the course of a game.

"He stood on his head and gave us a chance to be here," Kunitz said.

It's a quaint expression, but can the Penguins' nimble goalie really stand on his noggin?

"I tried, but it hurts the neck, so I don't do that anymore," he said, with a smile that is part disarming, part playful, and part the disguise of an assassin.

In the public prints and over the airwaves, Fleury was singled out as having been badly outplayed in two losses to the Detroit Red Wings. That comes with the territory in a championship round. But he picked himself up with two wins, earning honors as the No. 1 star in the series-tying Game 4.

"You need your goalie to be at his best, and Marc's provided that for us," Sidney Crosby said.

For as long as skaters have competed on the ice, this truth remains — the goaltender likely will be the determining factor in which team takes two of the final three games.

The spotlight always follows the man in the mask, dressed in all that armor, positioned at that spot on the ice marked with blue paint, guarding a four-by-six-foot net.

The Penguins drafted Fleury in 2003 to lead them to the promised land. In French, his name translates into "flower." Flower Power is not making every save but is making the key one against a key player at a key moment.

"He knows he has to play well for this team to win," said Ed Johnston, senior adviser with the Penguins and the last goalie to play every minute of every game for an entire season.

This is the kind of stage the Penguins had in mind when they traded up to make Fleury the No. 1 pick in the 2003 draft. (The other No. 1 overall picks in franchise history are Mario Lemieux and Sidney Crosby.)

He won his first NHL game as an 18-year-old against the Red Wings. But despite his cat-quick reflexes and Gumby-like flexibility, he was sent back to juniors and spent some time in the minors to refine his game.

"He fell into some bad habits," said hockey analyst Pierre McGuire, a former Penguins assistant coach who has seen Fleury blossom from his days in junior hockey. "Rather than relying on his quickness and athleticism all the time, he's now relying on fundamentals. But remember, the Penguins didn't have a goalie coach when he first came into the league. Now he's controlling rebounds a lot better. He's taller in the net."

There was plenty of criticism after Fleury had some pucks bounce off him for goals in the two losses in Detroit. But confidence in Fleury never wavered in the

room that matters most – the Penguins' inner sanctum.

"He's one of the main guys on our team," said coach Dan Bylsma.

Just go back to the first round when Fleury stole a game or two with spectacular efforts that frustrated the Philadelphia Flyers.

"We just couldn't beat Fleury," center Mike Richards said.

It's easy to forget that at age 24, Fleury is already playing in his ninth NHL playoff round.

"You can't buy experience. The longer you play those big games, the more the game slows down for you. It's starting to slow down for him," Meloche said. "And you know what? Marc-Andre is a dream to work with. Every day, we look at video. We talk on ice. He takes extra shots. He absorbs everything."

For his part, Fleury copes with the doubters and naysayers by ignoring them. He doesn't read the papers or watch TV.

"I play for my team. I don't worry about what's written or said," Fleury said.

It is said that goalies are a different breed, but they all have to be to able to stand up to sniper slap shots and peek through screens and keep battling during the scrums in the crease. Some goalies deflect pressure with a scowl or a stone face. Fleury flashes his pearly whites through that impish smile of his.

"I just enjoy playing hockey, I guess," Fleury said.

And now he has an entire Cup-happy city standing on its head. ◼

Marc-Andre Fleury has battled the expectations of the fans and media without complaint since he made his NHL debut at age 18 in 2003. Though he already seems to be an old salt in the Penguins dressing room, the star goalie is only 24 years old.

Operating in front of a goaltender with more quivers than last night's Jell-O and a defense that suddenly developed enough yips to jeopardize Marc-Andre Fleury even further, the Penguins made Game 2 of the Eastern Conference final the kind of offensive celebration that perhaps only they can engineer.

Evgeni Malkin got the hat trick, but Sidney Crosby and just about every other aspect of the Penguins' superior firepower exploded along with him to spray six pucks behind Cam Ward – and one in an empty net – powering Dan Bylsma's team to a 2-0 lead in the series.

"I think what you got out there was a just a great team effort," said Max Talbot, who beat Ward in the second period to erase Carolina's only lead en route to a 7-4 victory. "I think we really raised our play to another level, because we weren't satisfied with the intensity of Game 1."

The Penguins, whose 31 shots in Game 1 were four below their average, pounded Ward with 41 shots on the net in Game 2. Ten others were blocked. Eleven more missed the net. Chris Kunitz shot one that went in the net for the first time since like 1959. They outshot Carolina by 33 percent (42-28).

"I don't know if we frustrated them; they were battling and both teams got after it really good," said Crosby, who directed this pandemonium. "We're trying to keep the puck down low and create some things, and the longer you can keep it in there the more tired they're gonna get."

Two minutes after they dropped the puck for Game 2, Crosby accepted Kunitz's nifty backhanded crossing pass to the left of the Carolina net and flicked it past Ward for the first of four Penguins leads. Lest it get lost in last night's little blizzard of offensive hockey, Crosby had to his credit, at that moment, 7:42 p.m., twice as many points in these playoffs as any two Hurricanes.

You read it right.

Of course, you get nothing for that but admiration, but it left the pregame words of Crosby linemate Bill Guerin ringing in the ears.

"He was born for this stuff," Guerin had said. "He's a real leader. People don't know how much of a leader he is. He's the hardest-working guy at practice every day. He's different than everybody. There's something about him that just sets him aside.

"He doesn't take a shift off. When you have someone that talented, that strong, that determined, who just keeps comin' at ya ... "

There was simply no need to complete that thought at that moment, and the right words aren't necessarily sufficient anyway, but the sentiment was clear in the demeanor of Ward near the end of the second period, after Talbot erased the only Penguins deficit of the game with a slapper that trailed sparks from the left-wing circle to the back of the net.

Crosby with the second assist.

Flying down the left wing one on one with Carolina defenseman Joni Pitkanen, Sid wound up for a slapshot, started his swing, halted it, dragged the puck around a puzzled Pitkanen, and backhanded it on net with such authority that Ward nearly jumped out of his skin before controlling it near his navel.

Was it me, or as Ward dropped the puck on the surface to await the next faceoff, could the besieged Carolina goalie be seen shaking his head?

(Crosby's goal further necessitated this bit of book-keeping. His 13th of the playoffs was the sixth time in the postseason he had rapped in the first goal of the game, tying the all-time NHL playoff record set by Bobby Hull of the Chicago Blackhawks in 1962 and tied by Fernando Pisani of the Edmonton Oilers 44 years later.)

But as the Penguins surrendered lead after lead after lead, 1-0, 2-1, 4-3, every one erased by Hurricane force Carolina offense, it was apparent only that

Crosby would have to do more.

So he blasted into the left-wing corner after Joseph Corvo, knocked him off the puck, fell on top of him, scrambled to his feet, whirled away along the half boards until somebody in a white sweater had to do something.

Backchecking center Matt Cullen tripped him, drawing the penalty that invited the Penguins to snap a 4-4 deadlock. Cullen was livid, partly over the call, but just as assuredly with the frustration over Carolina's inability to deal with Crosby in its own end. It was that very frustration, by no argumentative stretch, that left

the Hurricanes so overtaxed on defense that there was insufficient energy to deal with a swooping, energized Geno Malkin.

Malkin got the go-ahead goal, stuffing in his own rebound to make it 5-4, then whipped a beauteous backhander by the unraveling Ward for the hat trick. "He's not the leading scorer in the league for nothing," Talbot said.

And Crosby's not the best player on the planet for nothing either. Together with Bylsma's excellent cast, on nights like this, they're just an awful lot to overcome. ∎

Carolina defenseman Joe Corvo was not the only Hurricane left on the ice by Sidney Crosby and the rest of the Penguins star-studded attack in the 2009 playoffs. Opponents came and went without being able to contain Crosby or Evgeni Malkin, with the two combining to skate circles around every team they faced.

Lemieux
THE SAVIOR

By Robert Dvorchak

Before Mario Lemieux, the Penguins were just about on life support as an NHL franchise. They had won a total of three playoff series in 17 years and never went beyond the second round. Ownership issues were chronic, and in the 1983–84 season, they finished at the bottom in the standings and in attendance.

After the Penguins made him the first overall pick of the draft on June 9, 1984, the savior had arrived. Tangible evidence came when No. 66 – *Nombre Soisante-six* – scored a goal on the first shot of the first shift of his first NHL game, finished with 100 points in his first season, and was named rookie of the year.

Oh, it took several more years to surround him with the supporting cast that could win championships. But Lemieux – whose name means "the best" in French – has dazzled both on and off the ice despite an extraordinary series of physical ailments during a 17-season playing career. Although he will always be remembered for his offensive prowess, he also recorded the two biggest saves in franchise history – saving the Penguins when he was drafted and then pulling them out of bankruptcy when he took control of the franchise in 1999.

The love of sports is seemingly part of the DNA in Pittsburgh, which embraces stars who come through on the championship stage. Not only did Lemieux bring the Stanley Cup to Pittsburgh in 1991 and 1992, he was awarded the Conn Smythe Trophy as playoff MVP both times. Little wonder that 66 Mario Lemieux Place is the mailing address for where the Penguins play and that his nameplate still adorns a space in the dressing room.

The mantle in his Southpointe home is decorated with prestigious hardware. Among them: six NHL scoring titles, three MVP awards for the regular season, four Pearson Trophies as the NHL's outstanding player as voted by his peers, an Olympic Gold Medal for Canada in 2002, and gold medals in the Canada Cup and World Cup. In conjunction with the *Pittsburgh Post-Gazette*'s Dapper Dan awards, fans voted him the most stellar athlete in the city's history.

As great as they are, those accomplishments have even more luster because of the obstacles Lemieux overcame in his playing career – surgeries for a chronically bad back and a bad hip, a bout with Hodgkin's disease that required radiation treatments, and a broken hand, among other ailments.

Not even retirement could stop him. After giving up the game and being inducted into the NHL Hall of

Mario Lemieux won and experienced just about everything during his playing career. One of just three Hall of Famers to ever play following their induction, he will be forever remembered in Pittsburgh for hoisting two Stanley Cups.

A hero and inspiration to any person who saw him play the game, Lemieux was struck down by illness and injury at the absolute peak of his career. He battled, battled, and battled more, returning every time to lead the franchise he will forever be the face of.

Fame, Lemieux returned to the ice in 2000.

He also pulled the franchise out of a second bankruptcy when the money he was owed by the previous owners helped him take over the team. It was hailed as the biggest save in franchise history and made Lemieux a savior for the second time.

Under improbable circumstances, his retired No. 66 jersey was brought back down from the rafters of Mellon Arena so he could play again. He had the distinction of being the owner of the team he played for.

At various points, he hoped to sell the team and retire to a quiet life with his family. But after leading a grueling effort to secure a new arena, Lemieux is entrenched as the franchise owner and guardian of its legacy.

"No matter what happens in the future, I'm always going to be a Pittsburgher," Lemieux said upon his second retirement in 2006. "My heart's always going to be here."

Lemieux's last season, abbreviated as it was, saw him skate on Sidney Crosby's line. The passing of the torch was more than symbolic. Lemieux's 690th and final goal was scored against Montreal on Nov. 10, 2005. Crosby won that game with a shootout goal.

The special bond between Lemieux, the Penguins and the city was underscored on Oct. 5, 2006, when his number was retired for good on the occasion of his 41st birthday. Crosby provided a lasting tribute in the ceremony at Mellon Arena.

"Speaking for the rest of the players, as long as that 66 hangs above us, we'll do our best to carry on your legacy," said Crosby, one captain to another. ▪

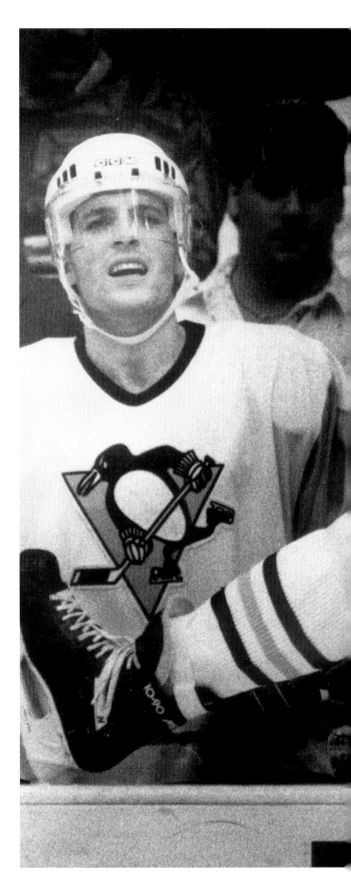

The fiery leader of his team, Lemieux missed many games over his 17 seasons but was never in the background. With three Art Ross Trophies and a pair of Conn Smythe's in his personal trophy case, few players can match Lemieux's achievements.

Fans score with their LOYALTY

May 6, 2009 • By Robert Dvorchak

Recalling his NHL playing days with Anaheim and Los Angeles, Dan Bylsma can say that the West Coast had good hockey fans.

But it wasn't until the playoffs started that he experienced the fanaticism that the Penguins generate – such as the citizenry in such a froth that fans swarm to watch games on a big screen TV outside the arena if NBC isn't involved in the broadcast.

"The fans and the city embrace their teams. They embrace their players. They embrace their coaches. They're vested. They're with you when you do well, they agonize when you're not doing so well. It's an awesome thing to be a part of. It's an awesome thing to see," the new Penguins coach said before the second round of the playoffs started.

"When you leave the rink, when you come to the rink, when you pick up the paper, when you walk the streets, the fans are living and dying with you. It says volumes about the sports town that Pittsburgh is and how outstanding our fans are," he added.

It also speaks volume about the Penguins, who not that long ago were experiencing tougher times. It's early May and the trees and flowers are in bloom, but ice hockey is bringing out the Penguins colors as conversations are spiked with references to face-offs and forechecking.

While the Penguins are prime examples of the bandwagon effect, hockey has always had an avid following in this town.

As one sign of vibrancy, the renewal rate among season ticket holders is running at 96 percent for next season – the final one before the Penguins occupy the new building going up across the street from the stainless steel dome. The economy is the worst that most people have experienced in their lifetime, but those who pay the freight have already anted up. Plus, the Penguins have a waiting list of 2,000 accounts representing about 5,000 seats.

"We're very fortunate to be in this situation. It wasn't all that long ago that we had our struggles here," said team vice president Tom McMillan. "This is an exciting young team the community has embraced, going through another playoff run with the palpable anticipation of a new arena in the wings. We're encouraged, to say the least."

Other signs are subtler. In a commercial by the TV network Versus to capture enthusiasm for hockey, one snippet shows the rabid Penguins fans waving their towels during a whiteout – a game when all fans are encouraged to wear white.

"Most NHL teams have fans that wave towels, but we have an inherent and unfair advantage in that department," McMillan said with a chuckle. "Our fans know how to twirl a towel."

That's a reference to the Steelers and Terrible Towels. It's true that the passion for the Penguins may not be as wide as it is for the football team, but the passion runs just as deep. And it never hurts to have Steelers as fans.

Drop in on a hockey game and you could almost hold a team meeting. Mike Tomlin, attired in his No. 87 jersey, attends games with his two boys. Kicker Jeff Reed dropped the puck at a game following the Super Bowl victory. Players from Hines Ward to Ben Roethlisberger are familiar fans.

But the Penguins make it a two-way street. During the football playoffs, goalie Marc-Andre Fleury came back on the ice for a curtain call wearing a Steelers throwback helmet.

"Pittsburgh is a football town and always will be. It's also a hockey town," said team president David Morehouse. "I'm from Pittsburgh. I follow the Pirates, and Pitt, and the Steeelers. Not to take away anything from other sports or other cities, but Pittsburgh is a bona fide hockey town. People are excited about this hockey team. There's a general affection for fans and players, and vice versa. That's part of the mystique of this thing."

The best marketing tool in sports is a winning team, which helps explain why the Penguins have sold out every game for two consecutive seasons. But not even the two-time Stanley Cup champions of 1991 and 1992 achieved such lofty attendance numbers.

The Penguins lead the NHL in merchandise sales among U.S. teams, and they get the most hits on their Web site. Having 13 NHL scoring champions in recent years tends to build interest as well.

For the season, the rating on Fox Sports Net Pittsburgh was 6.98 — which means the percent of households with

televisions that tuned in to the Penguins – eclipsing the record of 6.1 set last season. The post-game show with Jay Caufield does a 2.5, which is a higher rating that it was for some games a couple of years ago.

The ratings for the first round this year were up about a point from the 15.5 for the first round last year. Mario Lemieux popularized hockey in his day, and the torch is now carried by Sidney Crosby and his teammates. When he's not performing in hostile arenas – like silencing the Philadelphia crowd at the end of the last series – the Penguins captain gives back by purchasing a suite for needy kids or hand-delivering season tickets. He's also partnered with Reebok and Dick's Sporting Goods to provide 600 sets of hockey gear, from head to toe, for youth league hockey.

The Penguins have cultivated a younger following as familiar with the fast pace of texting and twittering as they are with how Evgeni Malkin stacks up against Alex Ovechkin.

The atmosphere in Mellon Arena is a far cry from the old days.

"There was nothing worse than a Tuesday night in February with the Oakland Seals coming in," recalled Dave Disney of Mount Lebanon, who has purchased season tickets every year since the team was founded in 1967. In his mind, the tent is big enough for college grads and Greene County grandmothers.

"The more the merrier," Mr. Disney said. "There were enough years when we needed people on the bandwagon or we wouldn't have a band. Quite honestly, I used to be the young guy screaming at the other team. I can't do that any more. My voice gives out. I'm glad to see the young kids come in. They scream. They provide energy. They're loud. I think the city has proven they'll support a team."